HOW TO REPAIR FOOD

"If this is coffee, please bring me some tea.
But if this is tea, please bring me some coffee."
—Abraham Lincoln

HOW TO REPAIR
FOOD

Tanya Zeryck and John and Marina Bear

TEN SPEED PRESS
Berkeley

Tanya Zeryck
For Max, Alexa, and Tristan, may they never need this book.

John and Marina Bear
To our mothers, Mary Dorrow and Tina Klempner, whose cooking
first inspired us to think about doing this book.

Published in the United States by Ten Speed Press, an imprint of the
Crown Publishing Group, a division of Random House, Inc., New York.
www.crownpublishing.com
www.tenspeed.com

Ten Speed Press and the Ten Speed Press colophon are registered trademarks of
Random House, Inc.

Originally published as *The Something-Went-Wrong-What-Do-I-Do-Now Cookbook*
by Harcourt, Brace, Jovanovich, New York, in 1970. Subsequent revised editions
were published in 1987 and 1998 as *How to Repair Food* by Ten Speed Press,
Berkeley, California.

Library of Congress Cataloging-in-Publication Data

Zeryck, Tanya.
  How to repair food / Tanya Zeryck and John and Marina Bear—3rd ed.
    p. cm.
  Marina Bear's name appears first on the earlier edition.
  1. Cooking. I. Bear, John, 1938- II. Bear, Marina, 1941- III. Title.
  TX652.B34 2010
  641.5—dc22

                        2010032188

ISBN 978-1-58008-432-1

Printed in USA

Cover design by Nancy Austin and Colleen Cain
Book design by Colleen Cain

Whisk image copyright © iStockPhoto/egal
Wrench image copyright © iStockPhoto/DNY59

10 9 8 7 6 5 4 3 2

Fourth Edition

CONTENTS

INTRODUCTION

There are thousands of cookbooks in the world, and they are all, at heart, the same.

They tell you how to cook.

This book is different.

It tells you how to correct mistakes. It tells you how to undo whatever it is you have done that you wish you *hadn't* done. It tells you what to do about fallen cakes, salty soups, burned stews, overcooked cauliflower, and hundreds of other things that can happen even to the best of cooks. It tells you, in other words, how to repair food. (Say, that would make a good title!)

When your car breaks down, you don't throw it away. You find an expert in car repair.

When your washing machine fails, you don't throw it away. You find an expert in appliance repair. And yet most people who have kitchen failures throw the food away. There is no need. This book is devoted to the art and practice of food repair.

Read the preface or introduction to your favorite cookbook. Chances are you'll find a paragraph something like this:

Each recipe in this book has been carefully tested for accuracy. It is important that you follow the instructions exactly. Be sure you measure the ingredients carefully and time your cooking precisely. This is the only way you can guarantee perfect results every time.

Fine. We agree. Makes a lot of sense.

But among all those thousands of cookbooks in the world, have you ever seen a single one that tells you what to do when:

1. The doorbell rings and, while you're signing for the package that just arrived, the cauliflower overcooks and turns mushy.

2. You set the burner too high because you're not wearing your glasses and the baked beans have stuck to the pot and burned.

3. The cheese you were going to put in the casserole has gone moldy.

4. The telephone rings while you're making the gravy and, by the time you get back, it's gone lumpy (the gravy, not the telephone).

5. You have to make sandwiches for the kids, the only loaf of bread in the house is stale, and the schoolbus is due soon.

6. The stew is simmering away, but when you sample it, it tastes more like junior-high lunch special than beef bourguignon.

7. You forgot that you put salt in the vegetable soup, then you put it in again, and now it's much too salty.

8. Your invitation said dinner would be served promptly at seven, it's now half past six, and you just discovered that you didn't put the potatoes in with the roast.

9. You went mad at the farmers' market and now you have five flats of berries sitting on your kitchen counter.

10. Your spouse unexpectedly brings home his or her boss for dinner, and there won't be enough chicken to go around.

And so on. In other words, those other cookbooks simply do not tell you how to correct mistakes. None of them tells you how to undo the damage that you, or the supermarket, or Mother Nature, or the cow has already done.

This book does.

This book tells you what to do when you discover that just about any kind of food, drink, or utensil is overcooked, undercooked, stale, spoiled, burned, lumpy, too salty, too peppery, bland, too spicy, too hot, too cold, moldy, frozen, gamy, fuzzy, mushy, too dry, too wet, flat, tough, too thick, too thin, wilted, fatty, collapsed, exploded, shriveled, curdled, cracked, scaly, smelly, greasy, dirty, stringy, twiggy, mealy, clogged, or stuck together.

This book is *How to Repair Food*.

It first appeared nearly forty years ago and it's still unique. There have been several major revisions. The first came when Marina and John's youngest (by 3 minutes) daughter, Tanya, said, "This book is so politically and nutritionally incorrect it's embarrassing." We took a close look and were amazed by how much our eating patterns have changed over the years. Remember when a "diet plate" was a scoop of (full-fat) cottage cheese, a hamburger patty (lots of protein for you dieters!), a slice of tomato, and a canned peach half? "You're right," Marina and John said to Tanya. "So *you* update it." And she did.

A decade later, we (and the fine folks at Ten Speed Press) agreed that it was time for another revision. This edition has been thoroughly revised and expanded. But the basics of kitchen catastrophes haven't changed all that much. Things still get overcooked, lumpy, dry, and stuck.

What *has* changed in recent years is a growing awareness of and concern with healthy eating. These days a healthful diet is almost a social responsibility, and so is the economic and ecological matter of fixing something rather than tossing it out. Thirty years ago you could pour hollandaise sauce on a skimpy pile of asparagus and your guests would think "haute cuisine." Nowadays they think "heart attack."

Our expectations about what food should look like have also changed, which has given us one more great option for food repair: presentation. Those four spears of asparagus can now be tied together with a strip of red cabbage, red bell pepper, a thin twist of lemon peel, or, what the heck, all three, and yet again your guests will think "haute cuisine."

So, then, this edition takes these matters into account, emphasizing healthier and vegetarian options. (Full disclosure: Tanya is a long-time vegetarian, and now a vegan. Marina and John are still omnivores but eat a lot less red meat than they previously did, and most of that is buffalo.)

The vegetable section has been expanded to reflect the wider choices available in many farmers' markets and supermarkets. A decade or two ago almost no one worried about running out of tomatillos, or what to do with an excess of asparagus from their community garden.

A Note about Cookbooks

While preparing this book we looked at more than two thousand different cookbooks to see what, if anything, they had to say about repairing food. Not one acknowledged the need to do so. They all just assume that everything will always be perfect. These books tend to fall into one of five basic categories.

First, there are the Businesslike Cookbooks. They have businesslike titles such as *Basic Culinary Techniques* or *Mrs. Rutherford's Cooking Academy Cookbook*. They simply tell you how to cook. And, of course, if you follow their directions, nothing could possibly go wrong.

Second, there are the Specialized Cookbooks: *The Cranberry Cookbook*, *The Romance of Radicchio*, *Cooking from the Highlands of Tibet*, *1,001 Tempting Recipes for Leftover Okra*. But all they do is tell you how to cook cranberries, or yaks, or whatever. Never how to repair things.

Third, there are the Expensive Gimmicky Cookbooks, made either to be given as gifts or to be left on your coffee table. No one has ever been known to buy one for personal use. Examples of this type of book are *Favorite Recipes of the Postmasters General* and *Armand's Café Boeuf Cuisine* (where all the pictures are full-page artsy shots of Armand's hands knitting together a crown roast or arranging the garnish on his Shanks à la Shanghai). These books don't help you when something goes wrong—unless you can be consoled by looking at glossy photos of magnificent food.

Fourth, there are the Anecdotal Cookbooks, which tend to be travel books, joke books, or autobiographies with some recipes thrown in: examples are *Through Darkest Venezuela with Sterno and Toothpick* and *Take It Off, Take It Off (It's Boiling Over)*, the warm, witty story of Zizi LaFleur, Queen of Burlesque and Queen of the Kitchen. Anecdotes aside, these books tell you how to cook, but never what to do when what you cooked needs to be repaired.

And, finally, there is the unending flow of Folksy Cookbooks, the result of someone finally persuading Aunt Bessie, or Mrs. Mugglesby of Daisy Hill Farm, to record for posterity all her famous receipts (which is the folksy word for recipe). So we have *Aunt Bessie's Own Cookbook* and *The Eatin's Good on Daisy Hill*. Presumably Aunt Bessie never made mistakes. If she did, she ain't talkin'.

How this Book Is Organized

The largest part of this book consists of an alphabetical list of foods and then, under each specific food, another alphabetical list of the things that might go wrong and how to repair them.

For example, we have:

ASPARAGUS
BLAND
FROZEN TO THE BOX
NOT ENOUGH
OLD
OVERCOOKED
THAWED
TOO MUCH

Of course, the subcategories differ for each food; no two foods have an identical array of potential problems. Some problems you run into may simply not be listed. There are two good reasons for this:

1. Not every problem has a solution—or has, in fact, even been identified. Who knows? You may be the first person in the history of the world to suffer from stringy yogurt.

2. Not every solution is known to us. We did a lot of research, both in libraries and in our own kitchen, but there must be some things we have overlooked.

If you *don't* find the answer to your problem in this book, you may well wish to improvise, bluff, or otherwise muddle through. To assist you in this process when the need arises (and it will . . . oh, it will), we have included a brief section entitled "How to Improvise, Bluff, or Otherwise Muddle Through." Here you will find some general ideas along with a list of basic ingredients for a kitchen "first aid kit"—foods that can be used in different ways to help solve a variety of problems. This section, too, has been substantially revised and expanded from earlier editions.

We also include some corrective techniques that apply not to a specific food or problem, but to a wide range of foods. For instance, there are things you can do about burned foods that work equally well with burned green beans, burned stew, or burned pudding. The same is true for frozen foods that have thawed out before you wanted them to. So, for advice relevant to these situations—burning and thawing—see Appendices A and B at the back of the book.

There are other appendices back there, too, dealing with measuring, pouring, the seasonal availability of foods, stain removal, and so forth.

Appendix F deserves special mention. Called "Problems with Utensils and Appliances," it deals with situations ranging from burned pots to clogged grinders. It even covers those handy utensils you carry around on the ends of your arms, describing what to do about burned, greasy, smelly, or stained hands.

Tanya did much of the work required to edit and revise this edition, with help, as needed, from her parents (who wrote this introduction). It was Tanya who years ago pointed out that our advice on improving bland vegetables often involves adding something to the cooking water at the *beginning* of the cooking process. But how do you know foods are bland until the end? (This is the sort of thing that is annoyingly common in cookbooks. How many times have you read a recipe for, say, a frittata that says to add salt "to taste" to the egg mixture? Do people really scoop up spoonfuls of raw egg to taste?) Let's deal with that one right here. Sometimes you don't know until you've finished cooking something—your corned beef, for example—that it's bland. We'll help you figure out how to serve it now, and also what you might want to do the next time you find yourself preparing the same thing.

One more thing. Into every cook's life there occasionally comes Total Failure. Sometimes twice a week. Total Failure is a different kind of situation from any of the others we discuss, so we've given it a special section, just before the start of the alphabetical listings.

We hope you'll never need to use this book—in much the same way we hope you'll never need to see a doctor or a car mechanic. But we also hope you will agree that in all three cases you're kind of glad they're there.

How to Improvise, Bluff, or Otherwise Muddle Through

This is the Great Encouragement section. This is the place you turn to when the main course has turned gray, when your dessert won't jell, or when there's a funny smell in the house and you discover that it's coming from the kitchen.

Or, more generally, come back to this section when you have a specific problem that isn't covered in the main part of the text.

Our message is take heart! When everything seems to be going wrong—or has, in fact, already gone wrong—it is still possible to snatch victory (and your dinner) from the very jaws of defeat and the garbage can. You need only courage, a bit of creativity (yours or ours), and a good set of first aid ingredients for repairing damaged food.

Here, then, is our suggestion for a culinary first aid kit, a list of supplies that should equip you to weather a wide variety of kitchen catastrophes. And in case absolutely everything goes wrong, it is even possible to create an entirely satisfactory dinner for four out of emergency supplies you have squirreled away just in case. See Appendix H for details.

The first aid items are listed in alphabetical order. Permission is freely granted to add, subtract, or modify to fit your own needs and wishes.

First Aid Supplies

ARTICHOKE HEARTS (QUARTERED): If you have room in your freezer, keep a couple of boxes of frozen artichoke hearts in the back corner. They are unusual enough that they look special, and they're one of the few vegetables that stand up well to preserving. If your freezer is full, you can stack a couple of cans of them in the back of the cupboard instead (be sure they're not the marinated kind, which usually come in jars). They make a great addition to a too-small salad and are part of the emergency meal in Appendix H.

BAKING KIT: Flour, sugar, cocoa, baking powder, salt, vegetable oil, and vanilla. We could have listed each item separately, but these are what you will need for the emergency dessert in Appendix H. They are also generally available in small quantities (in case you don't bake much), last for a very long time, and can be used for other things. Flour is handy for thickening soups and stews and fruit desserts. Sugar? You must keep some on hand if you're going to offer your guests coffee or tea. Cocoa, of course, can be used to make, well, cocoa (which, by the way, is not much harder than using any instant package, and is much tastier). Vanilla adds a homey and very appealing flavor to any dessert. Even if you're just making an instant vanilla pudding, adding some vanilla extract will make it taste more homemade.

BAKING MIX: There is good, old, reliable Bisquick, which also comes in a reduced-fat version, as well as convenient baking mixes available in your natural food store. With one of these in your pantry, you'll be comforted to know that you aren't more than 13 minutes away from home-baked goods like pancakes, cookies, coffee cake, quickbreads, and biscuits.

BAKING SODA: Never let your kitchen be without it. Besides its cooking, medicinal, stain-removing, and deodorizing uses (you probably already have an open box of it in the fridge), it is also the ideal kitchen fire extinguisher, especially for grease fires. Simply pour lots on a fire. *Note:* Trying to douse a grease fire with water will normally only make things worse.

BERRIES (FROZEN): Most of the first aid supplies on our list are items that might last you until Y3K without going bad, but this one is different. We recommend keeping on hand frozen berries. They'll only last for a year or so, but if you haven't used them for a while, you'll just have to make some berry pies, a berry sauce for your pancakes or ice cream, berry ice cream to go under your sauce, or some healthful breakfast smoothies. In the meantime, they're very handy to have around to make all those menu items we just mentioned. Nothing is easier while seeming gourmet than a homemade berry sauce for that gallon of ice cream you just pulled out of the freezer.

BOUILLON CUBES: Any bland soup or stew can be vastly improved with a bouillon cube. Just make sure that, if the dish you're adding it to is at all thick, you've melted the cube in a bit of boiling water first. (Finding a piece of bouillon cube in a mouthful of food is not fun.) And, of course, a bouillon cube is also the start of a pot of soup; just toss in all the sad leftover vegetables at the bottom of the veggie drawer (as well as some of the other things in this list).

CAPERS: So maybe they're not a usual thing for most people to keep around, but not only are they necessary for the emergency dinner in Appendix H, they offer huge flavor as well. Salty and briny, they add pop to sauces, stews, and many a salad. Mix them with mayo and pickles for a gourmet tartar sauce. Or sauté them in butter to top a fish fillet. Even canned tuna becomes a treat if you mix in a caper or two (or six). Or mix them with that can of shrimp in your emergency supplies for a gourmet snack.

CHEESE SAUCE OR CHEESE SOUP: One can is instant help for some dry casseroles. Pour it on vegetables. Heat it up and pour it on toast for instant Welsh rarebit.

CLAM CHOWDER: Find a good brand that's short on potatoes and long on clams. It makes a good first course when you're faced with less main course than you need, and it's not bad for snacks or lunch either.

COUSCOUS (OR RICE): Look in the rice section of your store for couscous. Chances are overwhelming that you will find a box of instant couscous, which looks like a grain but is actually a pasta. Buy it and save it, unless you're not familiar with couscous. In that case, buy two and try one. It's a great "underneath" for meat, fish, or vegetable stews. It's exotic enough that it looks special, but it tastes simple and supportive. Best of all, it cooks in only 5 minutes. If you can't find it (or you or the two-year-old you live with won't try new stuff), then substitute quick-cooking rice, which even comes in brown nowadays.

EVAPORATED MILK: Next on your shopping list is a 12-ounce can of evaporated milk. How many times have you run out of milk in the last two years? See? Use evaporated milk anywhere you'd use whole milk—in desserts, sauces, etc.—adding an equal amount of water (so a 12-ounce can makes 3 cups of milk). You can also use it to make a whipped topping. And there are low-fat and fat-free versions, too. Choose your favorite.

FOOD COLORINGS: Here's a big secret: a few drops of yellow in your curried rice or biscuit dough makes it look richer. A pallid soup can be reddened a little and made much more appetizing. (Sure, you could grate a little fresh beet into the soup, but do you have a fresh beet on hand? Fine. Then use food coloring instead.) And then there's the blue mashed potatoes and the green scrambled eggs the kids are still telling their friends about.

GARBANZO BEANS: Also known as chickpeas, these beans are one of the very few kinds of vegetable matter that are not diminished by the canning process. They are great salad and main-course enhancers, because they're filling and nutritious and interesting looking while being fairly bland and adaptable, tastewise.

GELATIN (UNFLAVORED): For thickening cool things, unflavored gelatin works wonders. Soften a package in $^1/_4$ cup cold water and add it to 1 cup warm liquid to dissolve it. Then add it to aspic, pudding, cooked pie filling, or whatever. It will even rescue a soggy croquette, if that's your problem (see "CROQUETTES"). It is also a pretty good start for a lot of fancy desserts. Check any good cookbook or just improvise.

HOLLANDAISE SAUCE (CANNED OR PACKAGED): These days, you don't need much. Everybody knows it's sinfully rich and difficult to make, so a graceful dollop over insufficient vegetables can make a big difference. The same goes for fish and eggs. Use it straight, or add a pinch of tarragon and you have a basic version of béarnaise sauce for meat, fish, or vegetables. Add some tomato sauce (2 teaspoons per little can or packet of hollandaise) and you have Choron sauce for eggs or meat. Add $1^1/_2$ teaspoons grated orange zest and 2 tablespoons orange juice and you have Maltaise sauce, which will turn the most tasteless fish or vegetable into something exotic.

HOT PEPPER SAUCE: Is there anything, with the possible exception of a hot fudge sundae—and even then we're not sure—that isn't improved by a shake of Tabasco?

LEMON JUICE: Keep a bottle of the reconstituted stuff in your fridge. Lemon juice livens up older vegetables and doubtful fishes. Use it whenever something is darkening that shouldn't, such as fruit slices, avocados, or parsnips. If you don't want the finished product to have a lemony taste, rinse whatever it is under gently running cold water before continuing. You can even make lemonade for unexpected company.

LENTILS: You can purchase these already cooked and canned or dry (in which case they cook up in half an hour or so). We prefer dried, as they are a nice way to thicken a soup (they suck up a lot of liquid during cooking). They can even *be* the soup. Cook them in broth rather than water to give them a nice flavor. Throw in some sautéed veggies (onion, carrot, and celery) and you have dinner. Cook them with less broth so they're more stewish and toss in some potato and sausage and you've got *another* dinner. Cook them in even less broth and toss with vinaigrette and you've just fancied up your salad.

OLIVES (BLACK, PREFERABLY KALAMATA): A bowl of olives is an instant appetizer. Mixed black and green (if you have them) looks good. If you'd like to make your kalamatas fancier, you can marinate them in olive oil with some garlic (roasted is nice), red pepper flakes, and herbs (try chives, basil, or cilantro). Or they can be processed with some garlic, capers, and olive oil for a tapenade (serve with crackers). They elevate a simple salad to something much more interesting. Chopped, they add flavor and texture to sauces, stews, hummus, and pasta dishes.

ONIONS (DRIED): No one ever expects to run out of fresh onions, yet everyone does at least 4.7 times a year. Dried onions are a natural for helping fill out anemic soups and stews (add 2 tablespoons sautéed dried onions for each cup of liquid). They will add flavor to almost any bland vegetable, make an interesting topping for a casserole when combined with crushed potato chips or cornflakes, or even make blah sandwiches unexpectedly good (how about dried onions, browned or not, with cheese, or peanut butter, or tuna fish?).

PARMESAN CHEESE (GRATED): The ideal hurry-up topping, Parmesan hides a multitude of sins when used as a topping for a casserole and tastes good on most cooked vegetables, fish, and poultry. Don't forget a good sprinkling on a salad that needs something.

PASTA: Keep some dried pasta on hand. For the dinner in Appendix H, we recommend angel hair, but having any pasta around can help you out. You can use pasta to extend a meal you don't have enough of: elbows turn chili into chili mac; with ditalini, orzo, or other small shapes, vegetable soup becomes minestrone; a salad supplemented with farfalle is an entrée (perhaps with some garbanzos for protein). Of course, it also makes a main dish on its own, with plain old tomato sauce and Parmesan, or with a number of other things on this list (garbanzos, artichokes, and shrimp come to mind).

POTATO FLAKES: Mashed potato flakes are not just for making mashed potatoes. They are a fast and nutritious thickener for soups and stews. Just add them by the handful until you've got the consistency you want. They are also a great extender for most vegetables. Chop up the vegetable (for instance, carrots, beans, or broccoli) after it is cooked and well drained. Combine it with an equal amount of reconstituted mashed potatoes. Top this with Parmesan cheese and run it under the broiler for 2 to 3 minutes, until the top is browned.

SHERRY (EITHER DRY OR AMONTILLADO): Like hollandaise, sherry is a gourmet touch that can turn a disaster into a triumph. It makes any stew, soup, or casserole taste richer. Start with 2 tablespoons in a four- to six-person potful, let it simmer (or bake) for a few minutes, and taste. You can sprinkle it on a variety of desserts, from pudding to cake. And you can always serve it straight (or over ice) to your starving guests while you're busy patching up things in the kitchen.

SHRIMP (CANNED): This is the basis for any number of emergency responses. It can be added to soup, salad, or casserole. It can inspire quick appetizers or make a good sandwich filling or a late-night snack.

SPICES AND HERBS: You can add basic spices or herbs to almost anything with some likelihood of improvising it, or at least making it more interesting. Everybody has his or her own basics. Ours are the following:

> chile powder
> cinnamon (try it in entrées as well as in desserts and drinks)
> curry powder
> fines herbes (the herb blend by this name generally includes
>   parsley, chives, tarragon, and chervil)
> garlic salt or powder (powder is stronger; salt is saltier)
> Italian herbs (such as dried basil, oregano, and rosemary)

freshly ground black pepper

red pepper flakes (gives most anything a kick)

We've recently found a Thai spice mix (made by Spice Islands) that does nice and unexpected things to savory dishes and a Cajun spice powder (Luzianne Cajun Seasoning) that is so good that it might be addictive.

The basic rule of thumb when using herbs and spices is to add 1/4 teaspoon for each pound of ingredients, and then start tasting. Use this amount throughout this book unless we advise otherwise or your own preferences say something else. Some foods will require much more spice than this; others will need less, especially if you use strongly flavored spices like cloves and saffron. Improvise and experiment with whatever you have on hand. And write down what you do, in case you come up with something great.

TOMATOES (CANNED DICED, PURÉE, PASTE): Tomatoes can be added to soups and stews to give them some flavor and color, as well as to add substance when you don't have enough. They can also be used as the basis for a simple but satisfying sauce (as in the emergency dinner). Tomato purée is but a few herbs and some garlic away from becoming a sauce. Diced tomatoes are a nice addition to a rice dish, which can become Mexican or Mediterranean or Indian depending on the herbs you add. Tomato paste can be added to many sauces to liven them up, from Thai peanut sauce to many stir-fry sauces, to gravy. Canned tomatoes can be a far better option than tasteless fresh tomatoes in the dead of winter.

TOMATOES (SUN-DRIED): If you can find the kind packed in olive oil, get those. The oil can be used in a salad dressing or a pasta sauce. Otherwise, purchase them in a plastic pouch and leave it unopened until you really need them. Since vegetables that can survive in your pantry in the long term are hard to find, you should get to know these. They taste good, and they're sort of the pimento of the modern age, adding the cherry-red bits in casseroles, the spot of color in the garnish, and the interesting flavor in the emergency meal salad.

VANILLA PUDDING (INSTANT): A dessert's salvation. You can pad skimpy pie fillings by using the pudding as a base layer, with the fruit on top.

You can use it as a sauce over insufficient quantities of fruit desserts or cake. You can even use it, we are told, to make vanilla pudding.

VINAIGRETTE: You should always have a salad dressing, or some good olive oil and vinegar so that you can make some. Almost any vegetable can be made into a salad in a pinch.

You may ordinarily keep some of these things on hand. Buy the others and tuck them away in an emergency corner of the cupboard. They all have a very long shelf life. Sometimes true happiness is remembering that you have a can of chickpeas stashed away.

Let us repeat, because we cannot say it often enough: improvise! That is the key to success when something goes wrong. Think of it this way: what have you got to lose? As far as we know, there are no two foods that, when mixed together, will explode. The worst thing that can happen is that a partial disaster may be converted into a total disaster—perhaps even a glorious disaster, one your grandchildren will remember and discuss with awe.

And you may have surprising success. Look, if the Mexicans can serve poultry with chocolate sauce and the Uruguayans can improve a steak by spreading peanut butter on it, surely there is something you can do with the quivering mass in your kitchen that looks like the poster from *Invasion of the Killer Casseroles*.

Total Failure

When you have a total, absolute, cannot-be-corrected, you've-tried-to-improvise-and-only-made-it-worse failure, there are three, and only three, paths open to you.

The first is to run yourself through with your sword. This may seem a bit extreme for a culinary bungle, but there is good historical precedent: the case of François Vâtel, steward to the French minister of finance under Louis XIV, whom many still regard as one of the top ten chefs of all time.

One day King Louis XIV came calling. Vâtel prepared a great meal, but the king's party was larger than expected and there wasn't enough food to go around. Some had to make do with boiled eggs or the like.

Vâtel was disconsolate, but he vowed to redeem himself the following day, which happened to be a Friday. Fresh fish was a rarity in those days, and Vâtel had placed orders with fishermen throughout the region. Late that night he was called to the kitchen to accept delivery from one of the fishermen. He did not realize that this was only a small part of his order. "Is that all there is?" he asked in disbelief. "Yes," he was mistakenly told.

One failure was enough. Two in a row were literally unbearable. Vâtel went up to his room and ran himself through with his sword. He was found dead a short time later, when someone came to tell him that the rest of the fish had arrived.

Now, whatever you've done, it can't be that bad, can it? So please, do not run yourself through with your sword. For that matter, don't even jab yourself with your shrimp deveiner. Try alternative two or three.

The second alternative is to whip up a gourmet meal in twenty minutes, start to finish, from a simple set of ingredients you already have on hand. This is entirely possible, but only if you have the emergency ingredients described a few pages back. If you believed us when we suggested you keep a kitchen first aid kit on hand, turn now to Appendix H, and you will find a pretty good dinner for four that can be made from scratch in a mere 1,800 seconds.

Don't forget to replace any emergency ingredients you may use. We don't want to sound too pessimistic, but, as Mrs. Vâtel may well have said to her husband on Thursday night, "Sleep well, François; who knows what may happen tomorrow?"

The final alternative is to give up entirely and let someone else do the cooking. In other words, go out to dinner. You can deal with the kitchen disaster tomorrow, which is, as Scarlett O'Hara said, another day.

ALPHABETICAL
LISTINGS

ABALONE: *see also* FISH AND SEAFOOD

TOUGH: After it has been cooked and you find yourself faced with several rejected portions of (terribly expensive) abalone chewing gum, you can still produce abalone chowder. Very elegant.

Abalone Chowder

³/₄ to 1 pound tough abalone
4 slices bacon, diced
1 onion, minced
1 potato, diced
1 bottle (8 ounces) clam juice

3 cups milk, or 2 cups milk
   plus 1 cup half-and-half
2 tablespoons sherry
   (optional)
Salt and pepper

Was this your usual breaded slice of abalone? If so, scrape off as much of the breading as you can (but no need to get it all; it will help thicken the soup). Mince the abalone (a food processor will help). Cook the bacon, stirring, in a saucepan until crisp. Remove and reserve the bacon. Put the onion and potato in the bacon fat in the saucepan and cook until the onions are golden. Add the abalone, clam juice, milk, bacon, and sherry. Heat to a simmer and cook for 5 minutes. Season with salt and pepper. Serve in warmed bowls.

Next time, you've got to tenderize it more thoroughly. There are two schools of thought on tenderizing. The first says to slice it as thin as you can into big oval slices and then pound it with a meat-tenderizing hammer until you can read a newspaper through it. The gentle persuasion school says that after trimming off the inedible bits, you should slice off the "handle" (where it was attached to the shell). You now have two pieces of abalone. Wrap one in a clean kitchen towel and pound it, firmly but not violently, with a rolling pin, working from one end to the other until it "relaxes." This can take a while. Check to be sure you're not whomping it to bits in there. Then do the other piece. Then slice it on the diagonal into $^1/_8$-inch strips. Good luck.

AGAVE SYRUP

NEED SOME, HAVE NONE: You can substitute honey, maple syrup, or corn syrup in your baking. In place of $^1/_2$ cup agave, use $^1/_2$ cup honey or maple syrup. You may have to adjust amounts if you are making a large batch of something. Substitute $^3/_4$ cup corn syrup for $^1/_2$ cup agave, but reduce the other liquids in the recipe by a couple tablespoons. Using sugar in place of agave syrup is not recommended because of the difference in moisture, but if you must, you'll need more sugar ($^1/_2$ cup plus 2 tablespoons to every $^1/_2$ cup of agave) and you may need to up the liquid in your recipe by 2 or 3 tablespoons. (Please don't blame us if the texture isn't great. We did say it wasn't recommended.)

ALCOHOL: *see also* WINE

For major problems with things alcoholic, please consult the telephone directory for your nearest AA meeting. Here are a few lesser problems:

BRANDY OR LIQUEUR WON'T IGNITE: It's probably not hot enough. Drain it off if it's feasible (don't worry if it isn't) and start with new alcohol. Most of the liquor will burn off anyway, so your guests shouldn't get too sozzled—at least not from this dish. Heat the alcohol for flaming slowly, over a low flame. (If it gets too hot, it may ignite in the pan before you've added it to the food. If this happens, just pour it on the food right away.) When it's hot, pour it on gently and ignite the *fumes*, not the *liquid*. Say, maybe that was your problem in the first place.

DRINK TASTES TOO STRONGLY OF ALCOHOL: We don't know precisely what this means, but some people, not all of whom come from Iowa, think they do. An obvious answer for a punch or other mixed drink is to add more of whatever your alcohol is mixed with. But you've probably thought of that and you're out of it. In which case, they tell us that floating a thin slice of cucumber in the drink (or long, thin slices of cucumber in the punch bowl) makes it less alcoholy tasting.

NOT ENOUGH: If you're stuck with a depleted liquor cabinet before dinner, try making quick punch out of fruit juice, whatever you have that's carbonated, and whiskey, rum, brandy, or vodka. Doctor it to taste with sugar, lemon, butter, rosemary, nutmeg, or whole cardamom.

If it is *between* or *after* meals, things are simpler. Instead of punch, you can make Irish coffee, hot toddies, or brandied grog. Be sure you don't ask people what they want. Come in with the stuff all ready and those who imbibe are less likely to refuse.

PUNCH TOO BLAND, MISSING SOMETHING: Assuming that what is missing is something other than alcohol, here are three seasonings that tend to give punch punch: cardamom, nutmeg, and rosemary. For a punch bowl, stir about 1 teaspoon rosemary, ground nutmeg, or ground cardamom into $1/2$ cup hot fruit juice. Let it cool to room temperature (or, if you're in a hurry, let it sit for 5 minutes and cool it by adding cold juice). Taste test it by adding a bit to a sample of the punch before you dump the whole thing in. No spices? A simple squirt of citrus will liven up most any punch.

ALMONDS: *see* NUTS

AMARANTH

STICKY: Amaranth can be served either firm and chewy (but if sticky is the problem, you're certainly beyond that) or as a savory porridge. So stir in some extra liquid (broth would give it a nice flavor) and you're done. You can instead choose to mix it with another grain (it pairs well with quinoa), which will reduce the stickiness. If you're hoping to avoid this problem next time, try cooking it in a double boiler (and keep a close eye on it).

ANCHOVIES

NOT ENOUGH: In salads, add the oil from oil-packed anchovies to the salad dressing. It will make the salad taste considerably more anchovy-ful (and also more salty, so be sure to taste before adding any salt).

In hors d'oeuvres, mash up the anchovies with cream cheese.

In sauces (like spaghetti or pizza sauce), add the oil from the can to the sauce (remember about the salt).

SALTY: Soak the anchovies in water for about 10 minutes and then pat them dry with paper towels. If you don't intend to use them right away, store them in a container with enough olive oil to cover them. (No olive oil? All right, some other kind of cooking oil.)

APPLES, COOKED: *see also* APPLES, RAW

BLAND: Sprinkle on some powdered ginger, mace, coriander, cinnamon, and/or add a clove bag (a few whole cloves tied in cheesecloth) to an apple dish and cook it a little longer. Or dump some caraway seeds (mixed with sugar), some fennel, or some grated lemon or orange peel down the hole of a blah baked apple and cook it ten minutes more. Or simply squirt a bit of lemon juice over your apples. If your cooked apples aren't overly sweet, brown sugar can also add a nice flavor.

BURNED: See Appendix A.

NOT ENOUGH: If the apples are going to be served with meat, augment them with quartered onions sautéed in a covered saucepan until soft (about 10 minutes) in a tablespoon of butter per medium-size onion. If you like, you can also add a handful of raisins that you have plumped in a cup of boiling water and then drained.

If the apples are for dessert, combine them with cranberries or any other kind of berries (yet another reason to make sure you have frozen berries!), pitted cherries, or canned pineapple. Or you can add fresh sliced pears when the apples are about half cooked, and vanilla extract and cinnamon to taste. (If you use underripe pears, you may have to add more sugar.) You can add canned apricots if you're desperate, but be sure to drain them well, pit them, and then rename your dessert, for the apricots will now be the dominant taste.

APPLES, RAW: *see also* APPLES, COOKED

BLAND: Dip sliced or quartered apples, peeled or unpeeled, in powdered anise. Or sprinkle on some powdered cinnamon, nutmeg, and/or poppy seeds. In a fruit salad, try mashed-up rosemary or powdered cardamom.

(Stir $^1/_4$ teaspoon of either into $^1/_2$ cup honey and spoon it over the apples. Honey too sweet? Use fruit juice instead.) Improvise!

DISCOLORED: Apples do this when their flesh is exposed to the air. Rub a little lemon juice on the exposed flesh. If it is already unpleasantly dark, cut off the dark layer. No lemon juice? Dunk the apple pieces in slightly salted water until you're ready to use them. Or, if the taste is compatible with the finished dish, submerge them in pineapple juice instead.

MEALY: There is no known way to unmeal an apple. No matter what you were planning to do, make applesauce.

TOO MANY: If you've overdone it at the roadside stand, you can always make applesauce (it's easy) to suit your taste, whether you like it smooth or chunky, spiked with cinnamon or with maple syrup. Consult a basic cookbook. If you've *really* overdone it or aren't a fan of applesauce, try this recipe for apple butter (and feel free to double it).

Apple Butter

4 pounds apples	2 teaspoons cinnamon
2 cups apple cider or juice	1 teaspoon ground cloves
Sugar (white, brown, or a combination)	$^1/_2$ teaspoon allspice

Preheat the oven to 325°F. Chop the apples into eighths (no need to peel or core them) and put them in a pot with the cider. Cook over medium-low heat, stirring occasionally, for about 30 minutes, or until the apples are really soft.

Strain through a sieve into a bowl, pressing on and then discarding the solids. Add $^1/_2$ cup sugar per 1 cup of apple glop. Stir in the cinnamon, cloves, and allspice.

Put the mixture into baking pans and bake until done. You can stir it occasionally, but if you forget it will still be fine. How many pans you use isn't important. The more apple in each pan, the longer it will take is all. When is it done? When it's the texture you like. We usually take a couple hours. And if you overcook it, as long as it isn't burned, just add some boiling water to get to the consistency you like. This is a very forgiving recipe. Then you can either can it properly (see a general cookbook) or put it in containers and keep it in the refrigerator for up to 1 month. (Or share it with people you like.) We like it not only on our morning toast, but on our morning oatmeal as well. And it's a delightful addition to a plain bread pudding.

APRICOTS

TOO MANY: They will keep longer if you store them in the fridge. If you are overrun by apricots, though, and need to do something with them, consider this recipe (which pairs nicely with yogurt, cottage cheese, ice cream, waffles, cake, or your spoon).

Apricot Compote

10 ripe but firm apricots (you can peel them first or not)
1/4 cup orange juice (fresh is nice but not necessary)

1/4 cup sugar

Halve or quarter your apricots and remove the pits. Place them in a saucepan with the juice and sugar. Bring to a simmer over medium heat. Reduce the heat to low, cover, and cook, stirring occasionally, for 5 to 10 minutes, or until the apricots are tender. The longer you cook them, the more tender (mushy, even) they will get. Serve warm or cold.

UNRIPE: Place in a closed brown paper bag overnight (or for a couple of nights, depending on how unripe they are). Add a banana to the bag to get your apricots to ripen faster.

ARROWROOT

NEED SOME, HAVE NONE: Substitute cornstarch. In most cases, you will use the same amount. In some cases, though, you may need to add a bit less cornstarch. Start with about three-fourths the amount of cornstarch and add more if your dish hasn't thickened enough after a few minutes of cooking.

ARTICHOKE HEARTS: *see also* ARTICHOKES

FROZEN TO THE BOX: Run cold water into the box. After a few seconds, the artichokes should dislodge themselves.

PICKLEY: Sometimes the marinade flavor is so strong it pickles your taste buds and gets in the way of tasting the artichoke. Soak the hearts in water for 10 minutes, and then, if you aren't going to use them at once, store them covered with olive oil (or, if you have none, some other kind of oil).

THAWED: If frozen artichoke hearts have thawed out and you didn't want them to, see Appendix B.

ARTICHOKES: *see also* ARTICHOKE HEARTS

BLAND: The best thing is a tiny, tiny, wee bit of dried fennel (about $1/8$ teaspoon) in the cooking water. Once the artichokes are fully cooked, add flavoring to the butter you dip the leaves in, like a shake of Tabasco sauce. Or use hollandaise sauce or aioli (very garlicky mayonnaise) instead of butter for dipping. Or make instant béarnaise sauce by adding a good pinch of tarragon to packaged hollandaise. Or use vinaigrette (3 parts oil to 1 part vinegar) on either hot or cold artichokes.

DIFFICULT TO DRAIN: Put something absorbent, like a washcloth or lots of paper towels, in the bottom of a bowl. Turn the artichoke upside down in the bowl. (Please clean the washcloth before using it on yourself. If artichoke balm were any good for us, you can be sure the cosmetic people would be selling it.)

OLD: If your artichokes have been around a while, add 1 teaspoon salt and $1/2$ teaspoon sugar to each 1 quart water you use to cook them. The sugar sweetens them just a tiny bit (what a surprise!), and the salt helps retain their color and flavor.

If your old artichokes look funny, try removing some of the outer leaves. They may still be just fine inside.

SEPARATING, FALLING APART: Once it has started, there isn't much you can do beyond handling them very carefully. A good way to keep it from happening next time is to wrap the artichokes in cheesecloth before cooking. We suggest you remove the cheesecloth before serving—and definitely before eating!

ARUGULA: *see* GREENS

ASPARAGUS

BLAND: Add bouillon to the cooking water next time. For now, sprinkle the asparagus with ground mustard seed or toasted sesame oil (along with some sesame seeds)—or use seasoned salt, or flavored butter, or tamari soy sauce. Or toss with chopped toasted nuts (almonds or hazelnuts are particularly good).

FROZEN TO THE BOX: Run a bit of cold tap water into the spaces in the carton; the asparagus should loosen up at once.

NOT ENOUGH: Not a problem. Asparagus displays beautifully in small quantities. If you're serving a special dinner, arrange the spears in a bunch or hold them in the middle and fan out the tips and bottoms. Tie the middle of the bunch together with a vegetable ribbon (a thin ribbon of cabbage, lettuce, red bell pepper, chives, or scallion—even a shaving of carrot will do) and arrange gracefully. If you're feeding family, make the following recipe.

Asparagus Risotto

1 small onion, chopped
2 tablespoons olive oil
1 clove garlic, minced
2 cups rice (no Italian Arborio rice? Use whatever kind you have)
3¹/₂ cups stock or bouillon (any kind)

1 lonely bunch of asparagus, cut into 2-inch lengths (set the tip pieces aside)
¹/₄ cup grated Parmesan cheese
¹/₂ cup heavy cream (or evaporated milk, or half-and-half)
Salt

Cook the onion in the oil in a saucepan until the onion's soft. Add the garlic and stir in. Add the rice and stir it over medium heat for about 5 minutes. Meanwhile, heat up the stock. Pour the heated stock into the rice (it'll sizzle a lot at first). Add the cut-up asparagus stalks (not the tips), stir it all together, lower the heat, and cook white rice for 15 minutes or brown rice for 30 minutes. Then add the asparagus tips, Parmesan, and cream and continue to cook until the rice is tender. Taste and add salt as needed.

OLD: Add a pinch of sugar (for sweetness) and $^1/_4$ teaspoon salt (to help retain color and flavor) to each 1 cup of cooking water.

OVERCOOKED: Easy answer—make soup. The very simplest way to do this would be to take a can of cream of anything soup, prepare it, chop up the overcooked asparagus, and combine it with the soup. No canned soup or want something a bit more homemade tasting? Make a cream sauce. (Any general cookbook—or the Internet—will have a simple recipe.) Chop up the tips of the asparagus and put them aside. Purée the rest of the asparagus stems in your food processor or blender. Add the white sauce. Put this lovely glop into a saucepan over low heat. Thin to the desired consistency with stock or bouillon and add the reserved chopped tips. Hoping to keep your heart healthy? Forgo the cream sauce. Purée the asparagus with broth and thicken as needed with potato flakes.

The following recipe is not only great for using up overcooked asparagus, it's a tasty main course.

Asparagus Timbale

$^1/_2$ cup minced onions
1 tablespoon butter
$^1/_4$ teaspoon salt
Pinch of nutmeg
Big pinch of white pepper
$^1/_2$ cup grated cheese
   (preferably Swiss,
   but any kind will do)

$^2/_3$ cup bread crumbs
2 eggs
1 cup milk
1 to 2 cups overcooked
   asparagus

Preheat the oven to 300°F. Sauté the onions in the butter in a skillet for 5 minutes. Put them in a large bowl. Add the salt, nutmeg, pepper, cheese, and half of the bread crumbs. Beat in the eggs. Bring the milk to a boil and stir into the mixture. Mash the asparagus into the liquid with a fork or potato masher until the asparagus is in small chunks. Grease a 2-quart mold or baking dish and coat it with the remaining bread crumbs. Pour the asparagus mixture into the dish. Put that dish into a larger pan on the bottom rack of your oven. Fill the outer pan halfway with boiling water. Bake for 30 to 40 minutes, until a knife inserted into the center comes out clean.

THAWED: See Appendix B regarding frozen food that has thawed before you are ready for it.

TOO MUCH: It freezes well. Blanch spears in boiling water for 2 to 4 minutes (depending on their thickness), plunge them into cold water to stop the cooking, drain, dry, and freeze in freezer bags. Or cook it all, refrigerate it, and use some the next day. It works beautifully chopped up in a quiche or frittata. Or make something such as the following.

Sesame Asparagus Salad

Chilled cooked asparagus
Lettuce
Roasted or fresh red bell peppers (or tomatoes, if you must)
Lemon juice
Canola oil
Soy sauce
Sesame seeds

Cut up the chilled asparagus and combine it with the lettuce and red peppers. Dress with a mixture of 1 part lemon juice to 2 parts canola oil. Add a dash of soy sauce. Cover with about 1/4 cup sesame seeds that have been toasted in a 350°F oven on a baking sheet for 5 minutes.

ASPIC: *see* GELATIN

AVOCADOS

DARKENING: Sprinkle lemon or lime juice on the exposed flesh; or cover it with a layer of butter, margarine, or mayonnaise; or press a sheet of plastic wrap directly against the flesh.

DIFFICULT TO PEEL: There is no easy way to peel an avocado, but many avocados are peeled unnecessarily. There is often no need, despite what recipes may tell you. Do this instead: Cut it in half lengthwise and separate the two halves. Wham the blade (not the point) of a big knife into the pit, twist it slightly, and the pit will lift neatly out. Now you can scoop the flesh out with a spoon or, for variety in salads, with a melon baller.

NOT ENOUGH: In a salad, avocado combines well with citrus fruit sections. In a tossed salad, don't worry. No one will notice. In a dip, fill it out with cream cheese softened with milk to avocado consistency. Vegans and heart-healthy folks might use silken tofu. When mixed in well and seasoned again, it will never show. If you're still worried, add a drop or two of green food coloring.

TOO MANY: If you are sick of guacamole, whole avocados can be stored in the refrigerator. They won't ripen (or overripen) as fast. To preserve the appearance and increase the longevity of sliced avocados, coat the exposed parts with butter, margarine, or mayonnaise (the thicker you smear the fat on, the longer it is likely to preserve the flesh) or press plastic wrap directly against the surfaces. Then you can keep them for days in the refrigerator.

If you would like to preserve your avocados for even longer, they can easily be frozen. Purée them, adding about $1^1/_2$ teaspoons lemon juice per avocado. Put the purée into a resealable bag and press out the air. It will keep in the freezer for several months. If you're still sick of guacamole, consider making this pudding. Yes, we said pudding.

Chocolate-Banana-Avocado Pudding

1 avocado, flesh scooped from skin and cut into pieces

1 banana, peeled and cut into pieces

$1/_2$ cup milk, plus more as needed (soy, almond, or coconut milk would also work well)

$1/_4$ cup unsweetened cocoa powder

2 tablespoons honey or agave syrup

1 teaspoon lemon juice

Purée all the ingredients in a blender or food processor until smooth. Add more milk if necessary to adjust the texture. Transfer to a bowl, cover, and refrigerate until cold. Eat.

Optional add-ins for stirring into the pudding just before eating: ¼ cup grated coconut, sweetened or not, 1 to 2 tablespoons of nut butter, fresh berries, and, yes, even chocolate chips.

UNCERTAIN QUALITY: Press the avocado with your thumb. If it dents easily, it is ready to use. If the grocer complains, tell him we said it was all right. If you've cut it open and wonder if the darker-looking portions are safe to eat—they are, but you'll probably want to mask them with an opaque dressing such as mayonnaise (or make guacamole).

UNRIPE: Seal the avocado in a brown paper bag and keep it in a warm, but not hot, place. If you need it to ripen fast, put a banana in the bag, too. If the avocado has already been cut open and found to be unripe, you can still coat the exposed surfaces (with butter or margarine—but not mayonnaise, please, because it will go bad too quickly) and close the avocado up around the pit. Put it in the paper bag and check it the next day.

BACON

CURLING: Once bacon is already fairly curly, the only thing to do is to put something heavy and flat on it—like a pot full of water—right on the griddle or in the frying pan. If it is already cooked and hopelessly curly, why not break it into small pieces and drop it into the eggs or whatever.

Next time, bake the bacon at 400°F for 10 to 15 minutes instead of griddling or frying it. If you bake it on a wire rack (or on your broiler pan in the oven), it'll be crispy and lovely. Baked bacon tastes just the same, but it just lies there, flat as a pancake. If you broil it, prick each slice in three or four places with a fork.

HARD TO CHOP: Freeze for 15 minutes until firm and chopping will be much easier.

ON FIRE: Small fire? Drop a pot or pan on top of it to snuff it out. Big fire? Pour on baking soda or salt. Lots.

STUCK TOGETHER: Method 1: Roll up the entire package crosswise. Unroll, and unless the pigs were fed on a diet of glue, the bacon strips should be unstuck. Method 2: Drop the whole stuck-together bundle onto the griddle, under the broiler, or in the oven. It will come unstuck as it cooks and the melting fat acts as a lubricant. You can then separate the slices and cook them one at a time.

BAKED BEANS: *see* BEANS, BAKED

BAKING POWDER

NEED SOME, HAVE NONE: For every cup of flour in the recipe, mix 2 teaspoons cream of tartar, 1 teaspoon baking soda, and 1/2 teaspoon salt. Use this right away; it won't be effective for more than a day or so.

UNCERTAIN QUALITY: Stale baking powder can ruin whatever you're making, but old powder isn't necessarily stale. Here is a simple test: Put 1 teaspoonful in a cup of hot water. If it bubbles a lot, it's good. If it doesn't, throw it out.

BAMBOO SHOOTS

NEED SOME, HAVE NONE: Presumably, you're stir-frying. (What else do Americans do with bamboo shoots?) If you have water chestnuts, they can be a good substitute. If you live in the West, you can use jicama, sliced into strips. You could use jicama in Maine, too, but you might have more trouble finding it in the grocery store.

BANANAS

BLAND: Sprinkle sliced bananas with spices, for example, anise, cinnamon, or nutmeg.

DARKENING: Coat banana slices with lemon juice. If they are already dark, slice them in half and arrange them good side up; no one will know the difference. An old wives' tale claims that bananas sliced with a silver knife don't darken as quickly.

NOT ENOUGH: You'll have to fill the dish out with something else. Ripe pears go well with bananas without imposing too much on the flavor or smoothness. In a salad, try a cantaloupe to keep a lonely banana company; the colors are lovely together and the taste isn't bad, either.

OVERRIPE, MUSHY: Of course, banana bread is the obvious choice, but if you're not feeling obvious, here are two very simple and good things made from overripe and mushy bananas.

Banana Milk

1 mushy banana   ½ teaspoon vanilla extract
1 cup cold milk

Purée all the ingredients together in a blender. Drink. Want to turn it into a treat? Add a scoop of your favorite frozen dairy dessert before blending and sprinkle cinnamon or nutmeg on top before serving. Want a frozen drink without the fat of frozen dessert? Freeze the banana in chunks first and blend it with just the milk and spices.

Roast Banana

1 mushy banana
Butter, melted

Peel back one thin strip of peel from the banana. Brush the exposed banana with melted butter. Fold the strip of peel back over the banana flesh, and/or wrap the whole banana in aluminum foil. Roast in a 400°F oven or over coals until the entire peel is black. Eat directly from the peel with a spoon.

TOO MANY (AND THEY ARE ALL RIPE AT ONCE): Well, you'll just have to make a banana cream pie. This can be absurdly simple if you use a store-bought pie shell, canned or dairy-case vanilla pudding, and spray-on whipped topping. See your favorite cookbook for homemade alternatives.

What, you still have more? All right. Mash them up, combine the bananas with lemon juice (1 lemon for each 6 bananas; or you can use that citric acid stuff groceries sell for home fruit processing), and freeze them in an airtight container or freezer bag. See, Chiquita, you *can* put bananas in the refrigerator! Now you have six months to find some interesting recipes for mashed bananas—banana cake and banana pudding for starters. Thaw fully before unwrapping or opening, or the banana will turn brown. (Although if it does, the taste is unimpaired.)

Does mashing them up sound too hard? Okay, peel them, cut them into chunks, and freeze in freezer bags. Those chunks can be thrown into milkshakes or smoothies and will add creaminess and sweetness (without the fat of ice cream). Cutting them still too much? You *are* lazy, aren't you? Okay, just throw the whole banana still in its peel into the freezer. When you take it out (the peel will have darkened considerably but the flesh inside will still be fine) and defrost (quickly done in the microwave), it will have become very mushy, making it incredibly easy to use for your banana bread (or cake, or pudding) with barely any effort on your part.

Or why not experiment with the latest in low-fat or fat-free baking? (For some readers, this hint alone is worth the price of the book.) Many cake, cookie, and muffin recipes can be adapted to eliminate from three-fourths to all the fat by substituting fruit purées (like applesauce or mashed bananas). Chocolate things work really well with bananas. If you also use one egg white for each whole egg in the recipe, you'll really be creating a healthier version of your goodie, without all those mysterious ingredients used in commercially available baked goods. It may take a little experimenting to get the proportions just right (start by using three-fourths as much mashed banana as butter or fat in the recipe, and add more if it's too dry), but you'll be doing yourself a lot of good!

BARLEY

BLAND: Cook with some bouillon for extra flavor. If you've already cooked it, you can dissolve a bouillon cube in as little water as will allow for dissolving (¹/₄ cup per cube if you mash it well), stir it in, then cover and let sit for 5 to 10 minutes. Stir again and serve. You can also add some sautéed or roasted garlic, caramelized onions, olive oil and lemon juice (perhaps with some parsley), or diced tomatoes (with or without some thyme or basil).

NEED SOME, HAVE NONE: Brown rice and quinoa tend to be good substitutes for barley.

TOO CHEWY: You probably haven't cooked it long enough. There are several forms of barley, from flakes (which cook quickly and are porridge-like) to pearl (which is possibly the most common and has a medium cooking time) to hulled (which confusingly can also be called dehulled and takes a long time to cook—as long as 1¹/₂ hours!). Whatever type it is, put it back on the stove, adding extra liquid as necessary. Next time, if you soak it overnight, it will cook faster.

BEANS, BAKED

BLAND: Stir in some ketchup or barbecue sauce or chile sauce or Tabasco sauce or brown sugar or rosemary or (what the heck?) all of them.

BURNED: See Appendix A.

NOT ENOUGH: Combine them with lima beans or kidney beans. Honestly, most any bean (besides, perhaps, green) will work beautifully: great northern, cannellini, navy, pinto. And this is a place where canned works very well. Add brown sugar, or molasses and sugar, or maple syrup to make them taste more beany.

SALTY: If they're very salty, about all you can do is add more beans (but not more salt, for goodness' sake). If they're just slightly salty, a little brown sugar and/or a little vinegar will tend to override the salty flavor.

TIME IS SHORT: Beans for baking should be soaked overnight. If you don't have time to do that, cover the beans with at least an inch of water in a pot, bring to a boil, then turn off the heat. Let the beans soak for an hour or two until they're nice and plump, then drain off the water and continue with baking as usual. If you don't have even that much time, add 1 teaspoon baking soda to 1 pound or so of beans, cover them with water, and cook on the stove over medium heat until they are soft, but not mushy, about 40 minutes. Add more water, if necessary, while they cook. Then drain off the water and bake as usual.

UNCERTAIN QUALITY: Dump the raw beans in water. The good ones will sink and the bad ones will float. Just as in real life.

BEANS, LIMA AND GREEN

These two kinds of beans are combined because most of the problems facing the bean world are shared by these two.

BLAND: A pinch of sugar in the cooking water helps bring out the flavor. On the plate or in the pot, try adding dill seed, fennel, or rosemary. Sage perks up lima beans ($1/8$ teaspoon in the cooking water for a cup of dried beans), and a sprinkling of sesame seeds makes string beans interesting. Toasted slivered almonds make string beans downright elegant.

FROZEN TO THE BOX: Run cold water into the spaces in the box and the beans will come out.

LOSING COLOR: When beans start losing color, and when it is very important to you that they don't, you can add a pinch of baking soda to the water. It will help them retain their color, but it will also extract some of the vitamins.

NOT ENOUGH: In many restaurants, you'll find something called Italian vegetables. Usually, but not always, this is a mixture of Italian beans, peas, and string beans. Very good. If you're desperate, even kidney or navy beans or chopped broccoli will do. Add a chunk of butter and cook together for 5 minutes so the flavors blend. Or do you have kidney or garbanzo beans (or both)? Then how about a three (or four) bean salad?

OLD: If your string beans or lima beans have been around for a week or more, add a pinch of sugar and $1/4$ teaspoon salt to the cooking water.

STRINGY: If your lima beans are stringy, you have more problems than this book can help you with. For stringy string beans, plunge them into boiling water for 3 minutes. Drain the water. They should be much easier to de-string.

THAWED: See Appendix B for suggestions on what to do with frozen beans that have thawed before you wanted them to.

TOO MANY: Lima beans reheat beautifully, especially if you brown $1/2$ cup minced onions and add them to the pot with a few tablespoons water when reheating. Crumbled bacon on top is a nice touch, too. Lima beans are also delicious roasted with olive oil, garlic, and sliced green olives. Yes, it sounds a bit odd, but it tastes fantastic.

Cooked string beans make excellent salad material when cold (as in a Niçoise salad). Before putting them into the refrigerator, dress them with a mixture of 3 parts oil to 1 part lemon juice or vinegar. Add salt and pepper to taste and, if you have some dill weed, throw in a couple of pinches. No dill? How about a dill pickle? Chop it finely and add it to the beans. (Remember that the pickle will add salt, so be careful in that department.) Those capers you have in your emergency kit will work, too.

BEAN SOUP: *see* SOUPS

BEEF: *see specific kinds of beef in the following categories:* CHIPPED BEEF; CORNED BEEF; HAMBURGERS; LIVER; MEAT LOAF; POT ROAST; ROAST BEEF; STEAK; STEWS.

BEETS

BLAND: Add a pinch of ground cloves or allspice to the cooking water— or use dried chervil (about $1/4$ teaspoon per serving). Or sprinkle the cooked beets with dill weed or mustard seed. Orange juice also works surprisingly well with beets. Squeeze a bit on top of boiled or roasted beets. Experiment with other seasonings. Beets are very adaptable.

DIFFICULT TO PEEL: Cooked beets virtually peel themselves if you treat them right. Put them in water, leaving about $1/2$ inch of stem and root on them. Boil for 15 minutes, then cool them under cold running water. When you cut off both ends, the peel should slip right off.

DISCOLORED: Add 1 tablespoon lemon juice or vinegar to the cooking water. Next time, do this at the start, just in case. It can do no harm.

NOT ENOUGH: Beets and beet greens are a good combination. Cook the beet greens separately and mix them with cooked diced beets. (Spinach, mustard, or other greens will do as well; in a pinch, so will lettuce leaves.) Add 1 tablespoon vinegar and 1 teaspoon sugar. If you are a bacon-fat saver, now's your chance. Add a scant tablespoon to the cooking water for a Southern flavor.

Another possibility is to grate raw beets, using the smallest holes on your grater. Pile the grated beets onto lettuce leaves and add a small quantity of vinaigrette to flavor them. Beets go nicely with carrots, so feel free to grate some carrots as well and mix the two. (Your carrots will turn a pretty pink.)

OLD: Add a pinch of sugar and a pinch of salt for each cup of liquid you're cooking the beets in. The former sweetens them back to their natural sweetness; the latter helps retain color and flavor.

SALTY: If pickled beets are too salty, soak them in water for 10 minutes, drain, and store them in fresh water. If cooked beets are too salty, drain the cooking water, replace with nonsalty water, add a dash of either sugar or vinegar—or both—and cook for a few more minutes.

TOO MANY: Of course, you can always make a salad with them (see how under "BEANS, LIMA AND GREEN, Too Many," and omit the dill weed). You can pickle them, too (refer to a basic cookbook). Or, better yet, surprise everyone tomorrow with this easy borscht.

Easy Borscht

1 package dehydrated
   vegetable soup
1 pound beef-stew-type beef,
   cut into small pieces
5 or 6 leftover beets

2 teaspoons dried dill weed,
   or $1/2$ teaspoon fresh dill,
   or 1 teaspoon dill seed
Dollops of sour cream
1 boiled potato per person

Make the vegetable soup using twice the amount of water called for. Simmer the beef in the soup for 1½ to 2 hours, or until it is very tender. Add the beets and dill and cook for 10 minutes more. Serve with sour cream on top. A boiled potato in each bowl makes this a whole meal.

BEET GREENS: *see* GREENS

BELL PEPPERS

BLAND: Sprinkle with celery seed or a tiny bit (⅛ teaspoon per pepper) of fennel.

NEED TO DESTEM: Instead of cutting around the stem, turn the pepper stem side down, cut most of the way through, break it the rest of the way, and easily break the stem away from whichever half it stayed with.

BERRIES

BLAND: Sprinkle them with brown sugar, confectioners' sugar, or one of the slightly sweet seasonings, such as nutmeg, cinnamon, or anise seed. If there is some juice, drop a whole cardamom or two into it during storage. A sprinkle of lemon juice (or orange or even lime) will perk up many a berry.

FROZEN TO THE BOX: Run cold tap water into the box and the berries will detach themselves almost at once.

LEAFY, TWIGGY: Sometimes there are lots of little leaves and twigs mixed in with berries, especially if you've picked them yourself. The fastest way to deleaf and detwig a large pail of berries is to pour them from one container to another across the path of an electric fan or a vacuum cleaner hose fastened to the blowing instead of sucking nozzle. Please aim the air in the right direction. Otherwise see a good first-aid text on removing berry twigs from the ear.

MOLDY: Pick out the moldy ones and taste a few of the rest to make sure that they don't already taste moldy. Next time you get fresh berries, you can follow food scientist Harold McGee's advice for inhibiting the mold: plunge the berries into 120°F water for 30 seconds, drain, and let them dry before refrigerating them. Better yet, freeze them (as described in "Too Many," below) if you need to keep them for more than a few days. But be aware that they will be mushier when defrosted.

NOT ENOUGH: Apples combine well with berries in pies, crisps, cobblers, and grunts (yes, that is a real dessert). Or use vanilla pudding to make a berry cream pie. Layer the berries and pudding into the crust, or mix them together and fill 'er up. Top with a meringue, and everyone will think that was what you planned all along.

For a shortcake, combine berries with fresh peaches, nectarines, or even pears. If you use pears, mix them with a sauce made from $1/4$ cup water, 2 tablespoons sugar, and $1/4$ teaspoon almond extract to give them more flavor.

OVERRIPE: Make fruit sauce. Clean the berries as well as you can, eliminating all the fuzzy ones. Mash the rest with sugar to taste (start with 1 tablespoon per cup of berries) and serve over pancakes or waffles. Or over ice cream or shortcake, or cream, or all three.

Or use them in a deep-dish pie or a cobbler. Overripe berries are very juicy, but this won't matter since you're only using a top crust.

SOUR: Stir them with sugar and allow them to stand at room temperature for at least an hour. Use about 1 tablespoon sugar per cup of berries.

THAWED: See Appendix B for info on frozen foods that have thawed out too soon.

TOO MANY: Clean the berries and spread them out one layer deep on a baking sheet. Freeze until firm and then pour them into some sort of storage container (freezer bags do nicely). Then, when berries are out of season, you will have the equivalent of fresh ones and not the sugar-soaked kind you usually have to settle for.

Another alternative is to make jelly or jam. Consult any good cookbook for directions. Making jam isn't nearly as hard as most people think it is.

WET: Nobody likes a wet berry. Line a big tray or baking sheet with paper towels. Pour the berries on it. Pat them gently with more paper towels.

BISCUITS: *see* BREAD AND ROLLS; MUFFINS

BLACKBERRIES: *see* BERRIES

BLUEBERRIES: *see* BERRIES

BOILED BEEF: *see* CORNED BEEF

BOUILLON: *see* SOUPS

BOYSENBERRIES: *see* BERRIES

BRANDY: *see* ALCOHOL

BREAD AND ROLLS: *see also* CAKES; COOKIES; MUFFINS; PIES

BLAND: Once it's made, you can't make the bread more interesting, so put interesting things on it. For the breadbasket at dinner, try making interesting flavored butters. Cream butter with herbs, spices, grated onion, or crushed garlic. If you're serving fish or poultry, try creaming orange or lemon zest into the butter. Serve the flavored butter in an attractive crock or small bowl.

If you have some really good olive oil on hand, consider serving that instead of butter, as many Italian restaurants do. Either serve each guest a small bowl of olive oil to dip the bread into, or provide a carafe of oil so each person can create a small pool of oil on a bread-and-butter (now a bread-and-olive-oil) plate for dipping.

If what you've got is bland sliced bread, toast it lightly and apply any of the above butters (and perhaps a flurry of sweet paprika). Cut the slices into strips, three to a slice, and serve it in a basket. They'll know you tried.

Next time, sprinkle on anise or toasted poppy seeds or sesame seeds before baking. Or sift some sage (1 tablespoon per loaf) or poultry seasoning in with the flour. If the main course is ham or pork, try adding $1/2$ teaspoon cinnamon and 1 teaspoon sugar per loaf to the dough.

BURNED: If you are baking or heating bread and it burns slightly, you can remove the burned spots with an ordinary kitchen grater. If there are lots of burned spots, you can cut them off and patch up the scars with bread ointment. Bread ointment is simply a well-beaten egg. Brush it on the wounds with a pastry brush and keep on heating the bread.

COLD: There are two ways to make cold bread hot without cooking it any more. For crusty kinds of bread and rolls, dip them very briefly in a bowl of hot water or spray using a spray bottle and toss them into a 350°F oven until they are as hot as you'd like. For softer breads and muffins, wrap them rather loosely in foil and heat for 5 minutes at 450°F.

DIFFICULT TO SLICE: Heat the knife.

To slice soft bread very thin, about the only thing to do is to freeze it, slice, and defrost it.

DOUGH DOESN'T RISE: When bread dough fails to rise, additional gentle heat often helps. If you have an electric heating pad, set it on low, put foil on the pad, and put the bowl of dough on the foil.

Another way to produce gentle heat is to put the bowl in the dishwasher and set it for just the drying cycle. (If you make a mistake here, see "Soggy," below.)

Or turn your oven to 350°F for 2 to 3 minutes, then turn it off, and put the dough in the oven. Did you remember to turn off the oven? One of the authors rises her bread this way and has forgotten at least once. (Anyone know how to rid a kitchen of the smell of melted plastic?) Another way to warm your dough in the oven—without turning the oven on—is to put it on a rack over a large pan of boiling-hot water (a broiler pan full will do nicely).

Alternatively, mix more yeast into ¼ cup warm water or milk. Let it stand for 5 minutes and then knead it into the dough, which should now rise. (However, see "YEAST, Expired.")

Sometimes the second rising just doesn't happen and you end up with a small, dense loaf. Slice it very thin and see if it's acceptable as bread. If not, make bread crumbs or small croutons out of it and make new bread using new yeast.

DOUGH RESISTS SHAPING: If it becomes tough and unmanageable, let it rest for 5 to 10 minutes, covered with a dampened cloth, while the gluten in the flour relaxes.

DRIED OUT: Wrap the bread or rolls in a damp towel and refrigerate for 24 hours. Then remove the towel and heat the bread in the oven at 350°F for 5 minutes. It should be restored to something close to its normal condition.

SOGGY: If sandwiches are needed and the bread is soggy, go ahead and make the sandwiches anyway, then grill the whole works briefly under the broiler. Unless you're given to making ice cream sandwiches on bread, it shouldn't hurt the ingredients.

STALE: Here are two fast techniques that often help revitalize stale bread:

1. Sprinkle ½ teaspoon water on the bread, seal it up in a brown paper bag, and heat it in a 350°F oven for 10 to 15 minutes.

2. Plunge the entire loaf (or rolls) into cold water for just an instant; then bake on a baking sheet at 350°F for 10 minutes.

Small amounts of very stale bread can, of course, be used to make bread crumbs in your food processor or blender. If a whole loaf should go stale on you, make a classic American dessert. Here is a basic recipe. Which is highly adaptable.

Classic Bread Pudding

3 to 5 cups stale bread (remove crust and dice the bread)

3 to 4 cups warm milk

¼ teaspoon salt

3 or 4 eggs

½ to ¾ cup sugar (white or brown)

½ teaspoon cinnamon plus ½ teaspoon cloves (alternatively, you can use ½ teaspoon nutmeg, instead of the cloves)

½ teaspoon vanilla extract

Zest of 1 lemon

Juice of ½ lemon

ingredients continued on next page

MERINGUE TOPPING (OPTIONAL)

1/2 cup confectioners' sugar

Pinch of cream of tartar (optional)

1/2 teaspoon vanilla extract

ADDITIONAL OPTIONS

1/2 cup raisins, dates, dried cranberries, nuts, chocolate chips, or any combination of these

1/2 cup drained crushed pineapple

1/4 to 1/2 cup orange marmalade, your favorite jam, or apple butter

1 to 2 tablespoons sherry or brandy

Put the bread into a baking dish. Combine the milk and salt and pour over the bread. Soak for 15 minutes. Separate the eggs. Combine the yolks, sugar, cinnamon and cloves, vanilla, lemon zest, and juice. Add the optional ingredients of your choice. Mix well. Pour over the soaked bread and use a fork to mix lightly. If you don't want to bother with a meringue topping, whip the egg whites until stiff and fold them into the mix. Set the pan in a larger pan of hot water (this is a kind of custard) and bake in a 350°F oven for 45 minutes to 1 hour. (How big is this thing? How deep is your baking pan? It should be set but not dried out when done.) Take it out to cool. If you want to make a meringue topping, turn the oven to 300°F.

Whip the egg whites until foamy and add 2 tablespoons of the confectioners' sugar per egg white, continuing to beat. Add a good pinch of cream of tartar, if you have it, and the vanilla and beat until the whites hold stiff peaks. Pile it onto the pudding about 15 minutes before you want to serve it and bake (no need to put it in the water bath this time) until lightly browned.

STUCK TO PAN: If bread sticks to whatever you're cooking or heating it in, wrap the whole works (bread and pan) in a dry towel while it is still hot. Let it sit outside the oven for 5 minutes. Unwrap and presto!

STUCK TO ROLLING PIN: If bread dough sticks to the rolling pin and you don't want to add more flour by flouring the rolling pin, put the rolling pin in the freezer until it is very cold, and then roll out the dough.

BREADING

FALLS OFF: This time, unless it came off in big replaceable slices, cover the whole works with a nontransparent sauce.

Next time, follow this six-step procedure: 1) Dry the object to be breaded. 2) Dip it in flour and shake off the excess, so there is only a thin coating. 3) Dip it in a mixture of an egg and a few drops of oil beaten well together. 4) Drop onto fine crumbs, to coat with a thin layer. Spoon crumbs onto any bare spots and pat them on. 5) Put on waxed paper in the refrigerator for 30 to 60 minutes. 6) Cook per the recipe.

Note: Breaded objects reheated in a microwave oven become soggy. Reheat such things in a regular oven, please.

BROCCOLI

BLAND: Mustard seed does interesting things to broccoli, whether it is put in the cooking water or sprinkled lightly over the finished product. A combination of tamari soy sauce and toasted sesame seeds will enliven either hot or cooked-and-chilled broccoli.

FROZEN TO THE BOX: Run cold tap water into the box. The broccoli will come up for air promptly.

NOT ENOUGH: A little hollandaise sauce will help. Everyone knows hollandaise is terribly rich, so they'll want less. Broccoli also pairs well with a nice rich cheddar cheese sauce—the same sort you'd be making for macaroni and cheese. Cauliflower is great with both broccoli and cheese sauce, so add some if you have it.

Or chop up the broccoli and combine it with soup, preferably homemade, but canned will do: cream of chicken soup or pea soup works well. Sprinkle with Parmesan cheese, paprika, and croutons and you've either got a soup course—if it's thin—or an interesting side dish, depending on the amount of broccoli you started out with.

OLD: When you cook old broccoli, add a pinch of sugar and a pinch of salt to each cup of cooking water.

OVERCOOKED: If you have an awful lot of mushy broccoli, see the recipe for overcooked asparagus. You may then prefer to call the dish Broccoli Timbale. Or you may call it anything you wish. There are those of us who think that naming dishes can be one of the enjoyable things about cooking.

SALTY: If you've put too much salt in the cooking pot, first change the water; then rinse off the broccoli gently under hot water, holding it in a sieve or colander, and return it to the pot.

If broccoli on the plate is oversalted, wash it off the same way in very hot water. A little lemon juice tossed gently with the broccoli tends to freshen the taste.

SMELLY: Is your broccoli smelling up the house as it cooks? Toss a heel of bread or a hot red pepper into the pot. Remove before serving.

THAWED: Please turn to Appendix B for one person's opinion of what to do when frozen food is prematurely thawed out.

TOO MUCH: Cooked broccoli will keep well for 5 days or so in the refrigerator. When you're ready to use it, it can be thrown into a quiche or a frittata with delicious results. Or stir-fry it with leftover rice, eggs, onions, tomatoes, and a bit of coconut milk for a nice Thai-flavored fried rice. If you suffer from low cholesterol, you can make the following recipe.

Savory Broccoli Custard

3 eggs
$1/2$ cup milk
$1^{1}/_{2}$ cups shredded
    cheddar cheese

Dash of nutmeg
Pinch of pepper
Lots of cooked broccoli

Mix all the non-broccoli ingredients together. (You can tell which ones they are, because they aren't green.) Lay the broccoli in a baking dish (the quantity really isn't important). Pour the cheese mixture over the broccoli and bake it in a 350°F oven for 30 minutes. Since what you are really doing is making a sort of broccoli custard, it is wise to rest the baking dish inside a larger pan with about 1 inch of water in the bottom.

BROTH: *see* SOUPS

BROWN SUGAR: *see* SUGAR

BROWNIES: *see* CAKES

BRUSSELS SPROUTS

Everything said about broccoli, with the exception of the suggestions under "Overcooked," applies equally well to Brussels sprouts.

FALLING APART: Remove the loose outer leaves and mark an X on the stalk end of each sprout (that is, the place where it was attached to the Brussels sprout tree, or however they grow) with a sharp knife before cooking. This will help the sprouts cook uniformly and be less likely to fall apart before they're done.

OVERCOOKED: Like building a perpetual-motion machine, devising a recipe using overcooked Brussels sprouts had long been thought impossible. We have finally cracked the O.B.S. (Overcooked Brussels Sprouts) barrier!

Overcooked Brussels Sprouts Recipe

Overcooked Brussels sprouts
1 tablespoon oil
1 tablespoon vinegar
(balsamic vinegar is
especially nice)
1 tablespoon brown (or white)
sugar

1 tablespoon soy sauce
(or $^1/_4$ teaspoon salt)
$^1/_2$ cup soft bread crumbs
$^1/_4$ cup grated Parmesan
cheese

Drain the overcooked little devils as gently and thoroughly as possible. Meanwhile, combine the oil, vinegar, sugar, and soy sauce in a small saucepan and bring to a boil. Sprinkle half of the bread crumbs in the bottom of a baking dish. Spread the sprouts over the crumbs. Pour the sauce on them, and then cover with a flurry of the remaining crumbs and the Parmesan cheese. You should warm this in the oven at 350°F, but since it's already overcooked, don't wait too long.

BUTTER

BURNING (WHILE SAUTÉING OR FRYING): Add a tiny bit of any kind of oil (except motor) to the butter when you see it is browning too fast. It doesn't change the flavor, and oil plus butter doesn't burn as easily as butter alone. Badly burned butter does have a distinctive taste, so if you have enough extra butter, why not start over? If you don't, pour off the melted butter and taste it. If it's truly unpleasant, then you'll just have to use oil instead, which will be fine but will change the flavor of the finished dish. If you think the butter that you poured off might be usable—i.e., it's not bitter and black—and you want to try for that butter flavor, mix with a little oil, put it back in the pan, and hope for the best.

NEED SOME, HAVE NONE: In baking, you can substitute 1 cup solid vegetable shortening plus 2 tablespoons water for 1 cup butter. You can sometimes substitute oil (one without a strong flavor) in baked goods, but the final product may be denser. If there are eggs in the recipe, separate them and whip the whites to add lift. (Drop cookies, however, may turn out cakier. Go figure. In this case, use a bit less oil than butter, say $1/3$ cup oil for $1/2$ cup butter.) If using oil or shortening and a buttery flavor is desired, add a few drops of butter flavoring. Of course, no one has butter flavoring on hand, so when you send someone out to get some, you might ask them to pick up a pound or two of butter.

Another approach entirely is the one detailed under "BANANAS, Too Many." If you're interested in low-fat cookery, it's worth considering.

For purposes other than baking, see the useful suggestion under "WHIPPED CREAM, Overwhipped, Separated."

TOO HARD TO CREAM: Shred the butter with either a grater or a potato peeler if you need only a smallish amount. If you've got lots of butter to cream, you can grate it with the grating disk of your food processor. In any case, warm the bowl you're going to be creaming the butter in by holding the bowl upside down over the sink and running hot water on the outside. If you're using sugar in your recipe, try heating the sugar before adding it to the butter.

Alternatively, you can soften butter almost instantly in a microwave. Heat an unwrapped stick of butter for 10 seconds on medium power and then let it stand for 5 minutes.

TOO HARD TO SPREAD: The problem is how to soften the butter without melting it. The solution is to cover the butter with a hot bowl for a few minutes: pour hot or boiling water into a stainless steel bowl, swish around, pour out, then invert the bowl over the butter. Or, microwave the butter on the lowest setting for 1 minute, and then let it stand for 5 minutes. If this is a frequent problem, check your local kitchen-supply store or online for a ceramic butter crock that keeps the butter spreadable but cool by storing it submerged in water on the kitchen counter, not in the refrigerator. Or, for the high-tech gadget junkie, there's the Butter Wizard, a temperature-controlled butter dish with a built-in fan.

BUTTERMILK

NEED SOME, HAVE NONE: In many recipes you can substitute $^1/_4$ milk plus $^3/_4$ cup yogurt for 1 cup buttermilk. Or stir a teaspoon of white or apple cider vinegar into 1 cup of milk and wait for 5 minutes. Don't drink it, but it's great for baking.

CABBAGE

BLAND: Try adding any or all of the following three seeds to the cooking water: dill, mustard, and sesame.

DISCOLORED: Red cabbage sometimes turns purple or blue during cooking. Add 1 tablespoon vinegar to the cooking water and it will turn red again.

NOT ENOUGH: Cold cabbage (slaws and salads) can be filled out with lettuce, shredded carrots, and diced celery, and it combines beautifully with pineapple (top with chopped nuts), apples (dice with the peel on, and add some horseradish to the dressing, starting with 1 teaspoon and tasting), and pears (add 1 teaspoon curry powder for each cup of pears to the dressing and top with a small mound of plumped raisins).

Hot cabbage can be sliced up into smaller pieces (assuming it was in wedges) and put into a baking dish. This is a messy job, but don't worry; it will come out looking all right. Pour cheese sauce or melted cheese over it all. Run it under the broiler until it just begins to brown. Have any bacon crumbles? Too bad; all right, decorate with nuts (such as toasted almonds), sliced olives, or good old paprika. Perhaps a shake or two of caraway seeds.

If you have tomatoes on hand, you might consider making the following.

Cabbage Ranchero

The quantities for this recipe are extremely variable, depending on how far you want to stretch your cabbage.

Onions, chopped	Ketchup
Butter	Chile powder
Tomatoes, chopped	
Cooked cabbage, cut into small pieces or chunks	

Brown the onions in butter in a large frying pan over medium heat. Add the tomatoes and cook for 10 minutes, stirring occasionally. Toss in the cooked cabbage, add a few tablespoons of ketchup and a rounded teaspoon of chile powder, and there you are.

OLD: Add a pinch of salt to each cup of the cooking water. This will help elderly cabbage retain what flavor it has left during cooking.

OVERCOOKED: Make cabbage soup. You can find a recipe in any general cookbook, or if you'd like life to be incredibly simple, just stir it into a can of cream of something soup made with milk. To make it a bit fancier, top each serving with a piece of cheese toast (like for French onion soup) or just a sprinkling of Parmesan or some toasted almonds.

Alternatively, drain the cabbage very well by patting it with paper towels after draining in a colander. If it survives this treatment, it is probably edible as is. Season it with garlic salt and pepper, and toss it with butter in a warmed bowl, if you do that sort of thing.

SMELLY: The old wives' remedy to prevent cooking cabbage from stinking up the entire block is to put a piece of bread, especially a thick slice from the end of the loaf, in the pot along with the cabbage. Rye bread seems to work the best, but any sort will have some effect in this antipollution campaign.

If the cabbage smell is already everywhere in the house, there is a good way to overcome it, if you like the smell of cloves. The odor of cloves tends to blot out the odor of cabbage. Produce eau de clove by simmering three or four whole cloves in a pan with vinegar in it. If you then decide that the cloves smell worse than the cabbage, you're out of luck.

TOO MUCH: For raw cabbage, wrap it well in plastic wrap or aluminum foil. It will keep for a week if it is fresh. So worry about it next Thursday.

For cooked cabbage, chop it up and refrigerate it. Tomorrow, make the following.

Bubble and Squeak

It's actually worth making too much cabbage (and some extra potatoes) just to be able to make this British dish. It's traditionally made with vegetables left over from your Sunday dinner, so there's no need to stress about the amounts. And feel free to throw in other cooked veggies like carrots, peas, and rutabagas. If the name doesn't work for you, perhaps you'd prefer to look up a recipe for a similar Scottish dish called rumbledethumps!

4 tablespoons butter
$^1/_2$ cup finely chopped onion
Leftover mashed potatoes

Leftover cooked cabbage
Salt and pepper

Melt the butter in a large frying pan over medium heat. Add the onion and sauté for 3 to 5 minutes, or until soft. Turn up the heat slightly and add the mashed potatoes and cabbage. Season with salt and pepper and cook for 10 minutes, stirring occasionally to ensure the potatoes and cabbage are thoroughly heated. Press down the vegetable mixture with a spatula and let cook until golden brown. Flip over and brown on the second side. Serve.

CAKES: *see also* BREAD AND ROLLS; COOKIES; CREAM PUFFS; ICING; MUFFINS

BAKING UNEVENLY: If you check your cake while it is baking (and you should, after 15 or 20 minutes) and the edges look done while the center is soggy, lower the temperature by 50°F. You may need to increase the baking time. Check again in 15 or 20 minutes (and later, check your oven control against an oven thermometer; it may be off).

BUBBLES IN THE BATTER: Put the batter in the pan. Hold the pan about 6 inches above the floor. Drop it. Do this three or four times, or until the people from downstairs come up to complain, whichever occurs first. The bubbles will go away and so, if you are lucky, will the people from downstairs.

BURNED: If the cake is fully cooked, either cut away the burned parts and cover the cake with icing (even if you hadn't intended to), or use a rasp grater to "file" away the burned spots. If the cake's too small now, slice it into layers and consider using a liqueur to sprinkle on the slices. Sandwich it back together with filling or frosting.

If the cake is not fully cooked but the top is brown, cut away the browned parts and cover the wounds with a first-aid dressing made from a beaten egg mixed with 1 teaspoon brown sugar. Brush it on with a pastry brush and continue baking (lower the oven temperature by 25°F).

CRUMBLY, CAN'T ICE IT OR SLICE IT: Freeze it. Ice it. Slice it. Thaw it. Go, team, go!

DRYING OUT: If you intend to use the cake fairly soon, brush some melted butter on the top and sides. This retards drying and also makes it easier to spread the icing on. If the cake is drying out in storage, put something moist in with the cake, underneath the cake cover. The cover should be as airtight as possible. The moistest thing of all is a small glass of water. A slice of apple or orange will do nicely, too. Don't forget to add water or change slices every 2 or 3 days.

Remember, too, that most cakes can be successfully frozen.

FLAT, SOGGY, FALLEN: If your cake is flat or soggy, you may have forgotten to put in the baking soda or baking powder. Or perhaps your baking powder had expired. An alternative explanation is that you may have added too much leavening (some is good, but more is not better).

Of course, at this point it doesn't matter why your cake is flat—you still have a flat cake. And sadly, no known remedial measure can correct this problem. (Forget the bicycle-pump idea. That only works in cartoons.) As Escoffier (or perhaps it was Joe at Le Greasy Spoon) said, "The cake shall never rise again."

But fallen cake still *tastes* pretty good, even if it looks dreadful. Use your imagination to come up with an interesting fallen-cake recipe. An obvious choice would be to spread it with jam, chop it up, and top with custard (or even pudding) and whipped cream. Voilà: a trifle! Or try the following.

Apple Moosh

Fallen cake   Whipped cream
Sweetened applesauce
  (canned or homemade)

Break the fallen cake into chunks. Mix with applesauce. Serve topped with whipped cream. No one will ever know it wasn't intentional. Is that too easy? Okay, you can:

Spread jam on the cake before you break it up.

Sprinkle sherry or liqueur on the cake before applying the whipped cream.

Plump raisins in hot water or warmed rum, drain, and mix in with the applesauce.

LOPSIDED: Check your cake midway through the baking time. As a rule, if it is going to turn out lopsided because of a defective oven or a tilted kitchen or whatever, turning the cake halfway around midway through the baking process should even it up. Check it again after a few more minutes. Keep turning, if necessary. If a finished cake is lopsided, slice the top flat and turn the cake upside down before frosting.

SLIDING LAYERS: Make sure the layers are completely cool before icing. If it's too late, consider sticking skewers vertically through the cake layers to hold them in place until things set. Save a bit of frosting to cover the holes. And remember to remove the skewers before serving. If you don't have skewers, we've seen uncooked spaghetti recommended instead, but if they break off, you're going to have to come up with a good explanation. Spaghetti cake, anyone?

STALE: Unfortunately, there is no good way to unstale a cake. Fortunately, a lot of dessert recipes work very well, sometimes even better, with stale cake. Check your big cookbooks. We suggest the following two possibilities for stale cake, one chocolate and one vanilla.

Chocolate Meringue Marvel

Stale chocolate cake, cut into 1-inch cubes
Egg whites
Sugar
Grated coconut or chopped pecans

Put the cake cubes in a baking dish. You can sprinkle with some sort of liquid, such as simple syrup, juice, or alcohol, but it isn't necessary. Whip the egg whites until foamy, then add 2 tablespoons sugar per egg white and continue to whip until the whites hold firm peaks (you can do this by hand with a whisk, but it will be infinitely quicker and easier with an electric mixer). Pile the meringue thickly over the cake. Sprinkle with coconut or pecans. Bake in a 300°F oven until the meringue is lightly browned.

Vanilla Rum Delight

Stale white cake, cut into 1-inch cubes
Rum
Thick vanilla pudding
Whipped cream

Put the cake cubes in a baking dish. Sprinkle with 1 tablespoon rum for each cup of cake. Spoon the pudding on top and stir into the cake. Chill. Serve with whipped cream.

STUCK TO CELLOPHANE WRAPPER: Packaged iced cakes tend to stick to their wrappers. To avoid that nasty possibility, hold the package under the cold water faucet for 20 to 30 seconds before unwrapping. (This works better if there is water coming out of the faucet.)

STUCK TO PAN: This is one of the most fertile areas for household hint thinker-uppers. Many techniques have been proposed, and they all have merit:

1. If the cake is still warm, let it sit for 5 minutes; it will shrink a little and may be easier to remove.

2. When you remove the pan from the oven, place it on a cloth that you have soaked in cold water and wrung out.

3. Loosen the edges with a knitting needle rather than a knife, place a wire rack on top of the cake pan, invert the whole works, and tap the bottom of the pan, if necessary, with a spoon.

4. Wrap the cake and pan in a towel as it comes out of the oven and let it stand for 5 minutes.

5. If the stuck cake is cold, reheat it for a few minutes.

Next time, don't use salted butter to grease the pan; it makes things more likely to stick. Instead, use unsalted butter, shortening, cooking spray, or, in a pinch, oil. But your best bet will be to line the pan with parchment paper, if you have some on hand.

STUCK TO ROLLING PIN: Wait a minute—what are you doing rolling out cake batter?

TOO SOFT; CAN'T ICE IT OR SLICE IT: Freeze it. Ice it. Slice it. Thaw it. Rah, team, rah!

CANDY

FUDGE, GRAINY: This can happen for several reasons: if you beat it at too high a temperature, or if it takes too long to cool. Is it salvageable? Maybe. You can try putting it in a saucepan with about $1^1/_2$ cups water and heat over low heat, stirring until it's dissolved and blended with the water. Increase the heat and follow the recipe again, cooking to the proper temperature, cooling, and beating again. If that doesn't work, remember that people never turn down fudge, even when it's grainy.

FUDGE (AND OTHER SUCH), TOO HARD: During cooking: add a little milk and cook to the proper temperature. After cooking: if the fudge won't pour, add 1 tablespoon milk and 2 or 3 tablespoons corn syrup; beat until smooth and pour at once. After it has cooled: put it in an airtight container. The fudge should become softer and more velvety within 24 hours.

FUDGE WON'T FUDGE: Fudge that won't fudge (fudge makers will know that feeling of beating a heavy, syrupy glop that just won't firm up) is most certainly not cooked enough. Scrape it back into the saucepan, add a teaspoon or two of water, and keep cooking, stirring constantly.

Divinity fudge cannot be made on humid days. If you've tried, and you have pools of sticky white stuff, scrape it into a bowl, beat in a few teaspoons of cream or milk, and use it as a great sauce on chocolate ice cream.

STUCK TOGETHER: If hard candies stick together in the jar or bowl, separate them by hand (unless you have a machine for the purpose) and sprinkle them lightly with granulated (or, better yet, superfine granulated) sugar before returning them to the container. (You can convert regular granulated sugar into superfine by giving it a whirl in your food processor.)

SUGARING: When chocolate candies start sugaring while cooking, add a little bit of milk and keep cooking until the mixture returns to the prescribed temperature. Crystals tend to cause sugaring, which is why many confection recipes tell you to wash down the sides of your cooking pan with a pastry brush dipped in water a few times during a long cooking process. You don't want to wash down the sides of a pan in which you're melting plain chocolate, though, or the chocolate will seize up into a lumpy mass.

CAPERS

NEED SOME, HAVE NONE: (But, of course, you have some in your emergency kit, so why are we even including this?) Anyhow, in some recipes it will work to substitute finely chopped kalamata olives. Or even pickles.

TOO SALTY OR BRINY: Rinse. If that isn't enough, soak in water for 30 minutes, then rinse.

CARAMEL

BURNED: Immediately dip the bottom of the pan in cold water to stop it from cooking. Now, how dark is it? If it's not dark black and smoking, it may be salvageable. These days "burnt caramel" is a popular flavor for sauces and ice creams. Even a very dark brown caramel may have a delightful smoky flavor that you'll enjoy, particularly if it's diluted by some cream. But if you don't like the taste now, you'll have to start over. And just so you know, there's a savory Vietnamese caramel sauce called *nuoc mau* that is cooked until the sugar is the color of molasses or coffee.

CRYSTALLIZED: To avoid big, crunchy sugar rocks from forming as you make caramel, make sure your sugar is fully dissolved before bringing the mixture to a boil. If you've already got a rock, do your best to break it up and keep cooking. It should eventually melt. (We say it *should*, but we once made a rock that never remelted. We served it as rock candy.)

CANS (KEY-OPENING TYPE)

KEY IS MISSING: Try using a regular can opener on the opposite side. Write a nasty letter to the manufacturer.

KEY IS STUCK HALFWAY THROUGH OPENING CAN: Holding the can with an oven mitt or a dish towel, try sticking a table knife through the hole in the key handle to get more leverage. (If you use your naked hands, you may as well get out the Band-Aids first to save time.) If this fails, and the contents can't be scraped out, hold the can over a bowl and use a can opener on the other side. Sometimes the newer cans aren't rolled on the bottom, though, and the can opener won't be able to get a grip. Then you may grab hold of the key with your needle-nose pliers and do your best to roll. Write a *very* nasty letter to the manufacturer.

Many cans that used to be key-opening (like those containing anchovies) now have pull-tab openings. They still get stuck halfway along. You can improve your leverage with two thick pads of paper towels (or two kitchen towels). Hold the opened end down with one protected hand and grab the whole pull-tab with the other. Growl loudly and pull. Apologize if you scared the cat.

CARROTS

BLAND: Try adding any of the following seasonings to cooked carrots, using roughly ¼ teaspoon per four servings: ground cloves, ginger, mace, marjoram, poppy seeds, or thyme. Consider ketchup or chile sauce over cooked carrots.

BURNED: See Appendix A.

NOT ENOUGH: For raw carrots, use with any other raw vegetable on a relish plate. Or shave them with a vegetable peeler and sink the peelings in a huge bowl of ice water. They will curl up, and when you have drained off the water they will look like three times as much.

For cooked carrots, cook them until soft and see the recipe below for what to do with overcooked carrots. Or mix them with peas (say, there's an original idea!), broccoli plus cheese sauce, or lima beans.

OLD: How old are we talking here? A little shriveled or limp, but basically intact? For raw carrots, soak them in ice water overnight. Adding the juice of one lemon or a tablespoon of vinegar to the water can help bring back some life, but isn't essential. But face it, once any vegetable gets slimy, it belongs in the compost heap.

For cooked carrots, add a pinch of sugar and ¼ teaspoon salt to each cup of cooking water.

OVERCOOKED: Try making the following casserole.

Potato-Carrot Casserole

Overcooked carrots   Cheese of any kind
Mashed potatoes (even
    instant ones)

Mash up the carrots with the potatoes. Pile into a baking dish, top with the cheese, and put under the broiler until the cheese melts.

See also the soup suggestions under "ASPARAGUS, Overcooked."

THAWED: See Appendix B for suggestions about foods that have been thawed out before you want to use them.

TOO MANY: Aw, come on. Carrots keep for up to a month when wrapped well in plastic wrap or foil. You're bound to think of something in thirty days. If they're already peeled, however, consider making a dip to dunk them in for an appetizer. Or make a carrot salad for tomorrow's dinner. You're having carrot salad *today*? Then cook them and see the next paragraph.

With a surplus of cooked carrots, consider the following.

Dilly Carrots

1 teaspoon dried dill weed or dill seed, or ³/₄ teaspoon chopped fresh dill
Dash of celery seed
Vinaigrette
4 cups cooked carrots

Combine the dill, celery seed, and vinaigrette. Toss with the carrots and marinate overnight, well covered. It keeps for several days and just gets more dilly.

Are you feeling really experimental? Make this.

Sweet Carrot Pudding

Cooked carrots
¹/₄ cup butter for every 2 cups carrots
Heavy cream, half-and-half, or milk (optional)
1 tablespoon lime or lemon juice
2 heaping tablespoons chopped nuts (any kind)
2 tablespoons raisins
2 or more tablespoons sugar
¹/₈ teaspoon almond extract (optional)
Whipped cream

Drain the carrots well. Mash them with butter to reach mashed potato consistency. (Add a little cream or milk if necessary.) Add the lime juice, nuts, and raisins. Sweeten until it tastes good to you. Add the almond extract, if you are so inclined. You can serve this hot, or eat it cold, topped with whipped cream or even frozen vanilla yogurt or ice cream. Talk about pumpkins and squashes at dinner and see if anyone figures out what you really made the dessert from. (They won't.)

CATSUP: *see* SAUCES

CAULIFLOWER

BLAND: Two seasonings that go well with bland cauliflower are mace (sprinkle on a pinch) and poppy seed (scatter 1 to 2 teaspoons per head).

BURNED: See Appendix A.

DISCOLORED: If the cauliflower isn't as white as you'd like, you'll have to cook it in boiling water (rather than steaming it) this time. Add a dash of vinegar after the water boils. It will whiten.

NOT ENOUGH: Cooked cauliflower is a strangely shaped (cauliflower-shaped, you might say) vegetable that doesn't really toss well with much. But if you've got a red bell pepper, cut it into strips. Combine it with your cauliflower florets and a good sprinkling of olive oil and roast at 400°F for 20 to 30 minutes, tossing every 10 minutes. Attractive and tasty. Or you can put any other vegetable (cooked) on the bottom of a greased baking dish, then a layer of cheese of any sort, then a layer of cauliflower, and a final sprinkling of cheese on the top. Use a tablespoon of the bottom vegetable as a garnish as fair warning to diners.

OLD: Add a pinch of sugar and another pinch of salt to each and every cup of water you use to cook it. They will help retain sweetness, flavor, and color.

OVERCOOKED: Let us tell you about overcooked cauliflower. It is an absolute godsend to dieters. You know all those things people make with white sauce (casseroles, gravies, timbales, etc.)? You can make awfully good, much-lower-fat facsimiles with overcooked cauliflower.

Keep cooking it until it is completely soft when you poke it with a spoon. Then mash it absolutely smooth (a blender or food processor will do this quickly). Add milk until you have the consistency of loose mashed potatoes.

Save this glop in the refrigerator to combine, for example, with defatted turkey drippings for lovely guiltless gravy. It's quite good served on real mashed potatoes. Or make the following dish.

Mock Potato Puff

Overcooked cauliflower

Onion powder (or finely diced
  fresh onion, sautéed until
  very soft and brown)

Salt and pepper

Parmesan cheese

Mash up the cauliflower, add the seasonings to taste, pour it into
a baking dish, top with Parmesan cheese, and bake for 30 minutes
at 350°F.

SALTY: If cauliflower is too salty on the plate, put it back in fresh boiling
water for 1 minute. If you discover you've oversalted the cooking water,
change it immediately.

SMELLY: Many hold that most of the smells that emanate from cooking cauliflower come from the water. And most of the smells enter the
water during the first 5 minutes of boiling. The solution, therefore, is
to change the water after the cauliflower has boiled for 5 minutes.

If it is too late for that, toss a piece of bread (preferably rye) into the
pot. Or make a solution of 1 part vinegar to 3 parts water, dip a cloth
in it, wring it out, and spread it over the top of the pot while the cauliflower cooks. Be careful not to let the cloth catch fire from the burner.
But if it does, it will certainly cover the cauliflower smell.

THAWED: See Appendix B if your frozen cauliflower defrosted itself
when you weren't looking.

TOO MUCH: Raw cauliflower keeps for a long time if it's cold and dry.
Cooked cauliflower can be used in salads the next day. Or cover it with
plastic wrap and refrigerate for two or three days. Then make the following dish.

Indian Cauliflower Pasta

Equal amounts of cooked
cauliflower chunks and
cooked pasta (a chunky
shape, like fusilli, radiatore,
or medium shells, is best)
Smooth or chunky peanut
butter, thinned with veg-
etable or chicken broth
to a gravy consistency

1/8 teaspoon cayenne pepper
1 teaspoon garam masala (an
Indian spice blend you can
buy ready-made or make
yourself)

Combine all the ingredients in a baking dish and warm in a 350°F
oven for 30 minutes. This works equally well with broccoli.

CELERY

BLAND: Raw celery is vastly improved by filling the trough with some
sort of delectable cheese goo like this one: caviar (red or black, cheap
or good) with sour cream or cream cheese, plus a bit of Roquefort
cheese. Soften the cheese with milk if it is too stiff. If you're feeding it
to children (or adults) who will turn up their noses at caviar, try peanut
butter instead. Feel free to add a line of raisins. (Remember the classic
"ants on a log"? It's classic for a reason.)

Cooked celery is perked up nicely if you add mustard or poppy seed
to the cooking water. (They cook celery? Sure. Consider it next time
you need another vegetable, on its own or to fill out a smaller amount
of something else.)

OLD: See "CELERY, Soggy."

SOGGY: Soak wilted celery stalks in ice water for 2 to 3 hours. If you
like, add 1 tablespoon vinegar or the juice of one lemon to the water. It
is said to help retain the flavor.

As an alternative, wash the celery, stand it vertically for 2 hours in a pitcher of cold water mixed with 1 teaspoon salt, in the refrigerator.

Here is one of the world's only recipes for hopelessly soggy celery.

Soggy Celery Dish

| Hopelessly soggy celery | ½ cup water |
| 1 can broth, any variety | Vinaigrette |

Poach the celery in the broth plus the water for 10 minutes. Drain. Split the stalks in half the long way. Cover them with vinaigrette. Chill in the refrigerator for at least 4 hours before serving.

CEREALS

BLAND: Oh my goodness, everything under the sun can be stirred into or sprinkled onto hot or cold cereals to make them more interesting. Just for starters:

Make hot cereal using chocolate milk instead of regular milk.

Add 1 teaspoon cinnamon, a dash of ginger, or a few cloves (tied in a cheesecloth so you can remove them) to hot water before adding the cereal.

Stir a cup of canned chopped fruit (per 4 servings) into hot cereal halfway through the cooking process. Add nuts, prunes, dates, raisins, currants, or other dried fruits to hot or cold cereals.

Plump dried fruits in hot water and let stand for 3 minutes for the fruit to rehydrate. Let cool before adding to cold cereal.

Put 1 tablespoon jam in a bowl, add a bit of milk, mush them together, and add to the cereal, hot or cold.

Put chocolate bits in oatmeal. (Think about chocolate chip–oatmeal cookies.)

Are you really experimental? The following recipe is a great camping breakfast for that morning when you can't face another bowl of oatmeal.

Layered Oatmeal

Brown sugar   Shredded cheddar cheese
Oatmeal

Put a layer of brown sugar on the bottom of a bowl. Carefully pile on
a thick layer of hot oatmeal. Top with a layer of shredded cheddar
cheese. If you can, cover the bowl with a plate or other cover and
let it stand for a couple of minutes to let the cheese melt onto the
oatmeal. You then eat the top savory layer first (if you like sharp
cheddar, this is especially good), and eat the bottom sweet layer as
your dessert.

Eat cold cereal with eggnog or instant malted milk.

Sweeten cereals with brown sugar or maple syrup or fruit sundae
syrup. Add ice cream, maraschino cherries, marshmallows, and/or
vanilla extract.

Go really nuts. Serve a tossed salad with a bland dressing (such as a
creamy French) and pour breakfast cereal (Kix, Cheerios, Chex) over
it, like croutons.

LOOSE: For hot cereal, add more cereal. For cold cereal, what in the
world can you mean by this?

LUMPY: Push hot lumpy cereal through a strainer. This will probably
make it loose. (Then, see "Loose," above.) Next time, start with cold
water and stir constantly, if you think it is worth the effort.

SOGGY: Somebody left the cold cereal open on the muggiest day of
the year and your cereal is limp and soggy. Pour it onto a baking sheet
and bake it for 2 or 3 minutes at 350°F. When it cools, it should have
recrisped itself. For a quick fix, zap it in the microwave for 30 seconds
or so, let sit for a minute, and enjoy.

CHARD: *see* GREENS

CHEESE

COOKED CHEESE THAT IS RUBBERY, TOUGH, STRINGY: This happens when there is too much heat. The excessive heat separated the fat from the protein in the cheese and the result is a Welsh rarebit (or whatever) that is rubbery, tough, stringy, and often looks awful.

This time, dump the cheese into a blender or food processor and blend at low speed for a minute or so to break down the rubberiness. Pour it back into the pan or, better yet, into the top of a double boiler and continue cooking. If the blending makes it too loose, add some browned flour (flour that you have browned on a baking sheet in a 400°F oven) until it is the proper consistency.

Next time, cook the cheese from the start in the top of a double boiler, making sure the bottom of the top pot isn't touching the boiling water below. It'll take a little longer than using direct heat, but it's foolproof.

DRIED OUT, STALE: If it is extremely hard, grate it (any cheese can be grated) and use it as a topping for vegetables or eggs or in a soufflé.

If it is dry but not all that dry, slice off the crusty edges (you can grate those) and either coat the bare edges with melted butter or wrap the whole cheese in a cloth that has been soaked in vinegar and wrung out. (Do you suppose that's what cheesecloth is really for?) Store the cheese in the refrigerator, in any case. If you have Parmesan or pecorino romano that's really too dry to use or you're too lazy to grate it, throw it in the pot when making soups like minestrone.

MOLDY: Cut off the moldy parts; the rest of the cheese won't be affected. To prevent mold from recurring, wrap the cheese tightly in plastic.

Note: Please do not try to remove the mold from Roquefort or blue cheese. It is supposed to be there. Thank you.

OILY: Wrap the oily cheese in paper towels; they will absorb much of the excess oil within 3 days or so. When the towels become too oily, change them.

SOFT, DIFFICULT TO CUT: Heat the knife or go out and buy a cheese-cutting gadget (a thin wire in a frame) for a couple of bucks.

TOO MUCH SUPPOSED-TO-BE-MOLDY CHEESE: Combine leftover blue or Roquefort cheese with an equal amount (by weight) of sweet butter. Add a dollop of Cognac and store in a covered jar in the refrigerator. It lasts nearly forever and is a great hors d'oeuvre served on crackers.

CHEESECAKE

CRACKED TOP: The cause is usually overbaking. Next time, make sure you remove the cheesecake from the oven while it's still a bit jiggly in the center. It will firm as it cools. A cracked cheesecake still tastes fine, unless it's *really* overbaked. If you want it pretty as well as tasty, consider serving it with a fruit compote on top. Or you can arrange fresh fruit slices in a pretty manner.

DIFFICULT TO SLICE: Dip your knife in hot water. Wipe dry. Cut. Repeat. You now have pretty slices of cheesecake.

CHERRIES

BLAND: For pies especially, it is nice if the cherries really taste like cherries. Surprisingly enough, they will even more if you add a few drops of almond extract to them. This is primarily for canned cherries but works with fresh ones as well.

PALE: In cherry pie, you want the cherries to be a nice bright red. If nature didn't do it, cheat just a little and add a few drops of red coloring to whatever you use as the thickening agent.

PITS: If you don't have a Tom Swift Steam-Powered Automatic Cherry Pitter, you can use a hairpin. Press the rounded top of the hairpin (a paper clip works, too) into the cherry at the stem end, then down and under the pit, and lift up. The pin and pit should emerge leaving the cherry virtually unharmed.

TOO MANY: Maybe now is the time to discover cherry preserves. Cherries are just about the easiest fruit to handle and therefore a good beginning lesson in your self-taught course in canning or freezing. Just think about Cherries Jubilee or hot cherry cobbler in the middle of winter. Home-frozen cherries last for up to a year—in other words, until the next cherry season. Consult any comprehensive cookbook for step-by-step instructions.

CHESTNUTS: *see* NUTS

CHICKEN: *see* POULTRY

CHICKEN LIVER: *see* LIVER

CHILI

TOO SPICY: Add more of something—beans, meat, and/or tomatoes. Add chunks of bell pepper. Even zucchini and cauliflower can taste good in chili. Just don't tell the Texas Chili League we said so. Another unconventional option is to add a can of refried beans. Or a dollop of honey. If you don't want to add something, you can try to unspice your chili. Peel and chunk several large potatoes. Mix into your chili and leave for an hour or so. Remove. Finally, you can dollop some sour cream or plain yogurt on top—that tends to cool the spiciness.

CHIPPED BEEF

NOT ENOUGH: Stretch creamed chipped beef by adding shredded cheddar cheese and serving it over biscuits instead of toast.

SALTY: Dunk it in boiling water for about 5 seconds. Rinse in gently running cold water.

CHOCOLATE AND COCOA

GRAY: The gray film or streaks that appears on chocolate is utterly harmless. It is caused by the chocolate being heated and cooled improperly, so the components separate slightly and a thin layer of cocoa butter "blooms" on the surface. You can melt grayed chocolate and use it as an ingredient, or just arrange to serve it in a darkened room.

HAVE ONE, NEED THE OTHER: Substitute 3 tablespoons unsweetened cocoa plus 1 tablespoon shortening for 1 ounce unsweetened chocolate, or vice versa. For every 1 ounce of unsweetened chocolate that you need, use 2 ounces semisweet chocolate and reduce the sugar in the recipe by 2 tablespoons. For every 1 ounce of semisweet chocolate that you need, use 1 ounce unsweetened plus 1 tablespoon sugar. Semisweet and bittersweet chocolate can be used interchangeably.

SCUM OR SKIN ON THE SURFACE OF DRINKING COCOA: Remove it with a cold spoon; then float a marshmallow on the top to keep the skin from reappearing.

STIFFENED UP: Water droplets, high temperature, and quirks of the chocolate sometimes cause melting chocolate to go stiff in the pan. The best rescue remedy is a teaspoon of vegetable shortening stirred in. Add more, if needed, to bring the chocolate to the desired consistency. Butter, which contains some water, will not work as well. Cream, however, may work. Whisk the mixture in a double boiler, while stirring gently, until the chocolate is smooth. You will have made a ganache (with which there are many delicious things one can do, such as pour over ice cream or eat with a spoon), but the chocolate may no longer be usable in the recipe that you intended to make.

CHOCOLATE GANACHE

TOO HARD: Place the bowl over a pan of hot water and stir gently until reheated.

TOO SOFT: It's too warm. Ganache needs time to cool to get to spreading consistency. If you don't have time, put the bowl of ganache over a bowl of ice and stir continuously until it reaches the proper consistency. If you don't have even that much time, decide it's a glaze and pour it over whatever you were planning to spread it on.

CHOCOLATE SAUCE: *see* SAUCES

CLAMS

CAN'T SHUCK: There is a long and involved procedure used by purists. You may be blackballed from the Clam Fanciers League for the following, but it works nicely, thank you: Drop the clams four at a time into boiling water. After 15 seconds, remove the clams from the water and slip a knife between the shells. The water relaxes the muscle that is holding them shut. Alternatively, they may shuck more easily when cold. Refrigerate them for an hour or so and try again.

SANDY, GRITTY: Sprinkle the clams with lots of cornmeal. Then pour on enough water to cover them. Wait for 3 hours. They will have expelled the sand and grit. Wouldn't you in a similar situation?

UNCERTAIN QUALITY: It is always safest to buy clams in the shell. Be suspicious of broken shells or ones that aren't tightly closed. If in doubt, dump clams into cold water and discard any that float. When cooking, any clams that don't open should also be discarded.

COCOA: *see* CHOCOLATE AND COCOA

COCONUTS

CAN'T OPEN: Method 1: Pierce the softest of the three or more "eyes" with an ice pick or skewer, drain out the water, and crack the shell with a hammer. If you can't get an ice pick through the eye, use a drill bit in an electric screwdriver (*not* an electric drill; it'll go too fast and grab the coconut, which makes a dangerous projectile). Method 2: Bake the coconut for 20 minutes at 300°F. By the end of this time, it will have cracked itself open, or just a light tap on the noggin (of the coconut) will do the job.

DRIED UP: Put the coconut meat in a bowl, cover it with cow's milk, and refrigerate for 1 hour. Press the meat dry in a strainer. (The milk can then be used for drinking or cooking.) A small amount of warm water can also soften your coconut, but it won't be as tasty as the milk when you're done.

If you have time, put the coconut in an airtight container in the refrigerator with a slice of fresh bread for 3 days, at the end of which time you will have fresh coconut and stale bread.

STALE SHREDDED COCONUT: Method 1: Soak it in cow's milk plus a dash of sugar for 3 minutes. Method 2: Hold it in a sieve over boiling water until it is as moist as you would like.

COFFEE

CLOUDY: Add eggshells to the coffee while reheating it. Strain before drinking.

NOT ENOUGH: Company's coming any minute and you're nearly out of coffee. Make mocha and you can serve six people with 2 cups of coffee. Here's how.

Mocha

⅓ cup unsweetened cocoa
3 cups warm (not boiling) milk
2 cups brewed coffee

¼ cup sugar, or more to taste
Rum or brandy (optional)
Dash of cinnamon

Add the cocoa and the warmed milk to the coffee. Sweeten to taste. A glug of rum or brandy and a flurry of cinnamon can turn a potential disaster into an occasion.

For after dinner, try Café Brûlot. Three cups of coffee will serve six people.

Café Brûlot

¾ cup brandy (or a mixture of rum and brandy)
6 cloves

2 tablespoons sugar
A few strips of orange peel
3 cups brewed coffee

Drag out the chafing dish, or herd everybody into the kitchen; this is too spectacular to be missed. In the chafing dish, heat the brandy, cloves, sugar, and orange peel. When it is nice and hot, ignite the vapors. Slowly add the 3 cups coffee to the flaming mixture, stirring slowly as you do. Serve in your smallest cups; this is supposed to be drunk from a demitasse.

OVERCOOKED: A tiny pinch of salt is said by some to take away the bitter taste of overcooked coffee.

TOO HOT: If you overheat coffee on a regular basis, why not keep a small bowl of frozen coffee cubes in the freezer? (See "Too Much," below.)

TOO MUCH: You made an entire pot and it didn't get drunk? Put the leftovers in ice cubes trays and use to make iced coffee that won't get watered down. If you'd rather use it up (or your freezer is too full), make milk shakes with coffee instead of milk. Or use as your liquid in baked goods. It makes brownies taste divine and adds interest to gingerbread.

COLESLAW: *see* CABBAGE

CONSOMMÉ: *see* SOUPS

COOKIES: *see also* CAKES; MUFFINS

BLAND: After baking (and tasting) the cookies, try brushing with a thin glaze made of confectioners' sugar and milk and sprinkle with small amounts of anise seed, cumin, cinnamon, ginger, or nutmeg. Or spread them with peanut butter and top with cake decorations. Or make sandwich cookies: use any kind of jam or fudge for a filling. Do you have chocolate chips on hand? Melt them and spread on for filling. Or make the following frosting.

Orange–Cream Cheese Frosting

3 ounces cream cheese,
   at room temperature
1 tablespoon orange juice

1 teaspoon vanilla extract
3 cups sifted confectioners'
   sugar

Cream the cream cheese until it is soft. Beat in the orange juice and vanilla. Add the sugar gradually, beating constantly. Spread on the cookies.

Or brush the tops of bland cookies with one egg white, beaten until foamy with 1 tablespoon good sweet sherry, and sprinkle with slivered almonds. Broil for 1 minute to set the nuts.

Or glue a flat chocolate wafer to the middle of the cookies with a dot of frosting, or by laying the chocolate wafers on the cookies and putting them (carefully) into a 400°F oven for just a minute to let the wafers melt slightly and adhere themselves to the cookies.

BURNED (OR BURNING): Cookies made on brown (generally nonstick) baking sheets and/or baking sheets with sides are more likely to burn. Next time, use the flat shiny ones.

If the sheet is half or less full of cookies, it may absorb too much heat and get too hot. Put an inverted baking pan on the empty half.

If you have have cookies with burned bottoms, cut or grate the bottoms off; the tops will taste fine. But they won't be pretty. So if you prefer, crumble them up and mix them in ice cream or crush them into crumbs and use them to make a pie shell. (And fill the shell with the cookied ice cream to make a double cookie ice cream pie.)

CRISP: Cookies that are too crisp will usually decrisp themselves if stored in an airtight container for at least 24 hours. Adding a couple slices of apple or a slice of bread can help.

CRUMBLY DOUGH: If the cookie dough is too crumbly but you don't want to add more moisture, try letting the dough stand at room temperature for 30 minutes, covered with a slightly dampened cloth. If that doesn't work, ask yourself why you don't want to add more moisture. A tablespoon or so of milk can be a very helpful thing.

HARD: Cookies that are hard will soften if stored in an airtight container with something from which they can absorb moisture. A glass of water does nicely; so does a slice or two of fresh bread.

SPREADING PROBLEMS: If cookie dough doesn't spread out satisfactorily before or during baking, use something cold and smooth to flatten out each cookie with a rotary motion. Suggested cold and smooth thing number 1: a spoon dipped in cold water. Suggested cold and smooth thing number 2: an ice cube wrapped in a smooth cloth or plastic wrap. If, however, it spreads too much, the problem may well be that the baking sheet is too warm. For the next batch, turn the sheet over and run cold water on the back (no need to dry it). Then put the cookies to cook on the other side. If your cookies are still spreading too much, try one of these options: Add a bit more flour to your dough. Or refrigerate your dough for an hour or so and try again.

STUCK TO BAKING SHEET: Run the baking sheet over a hot burner on the range. Or wrap the whole works in a towel as it comes hot from the oven and let it stand for 5 minutes. Sometimes greasing the spatula helps.

STUCK TO HANDS: Wash your hands in cold water. Or juggle a handful of ice cubes for as long as you can bear it. The dough won't stick.

STUCK TO ROLLING PIN: If you don't want to add more flour to the dough by flouring the pin, chill the pin in the freezer and the dough won't stick.

CORN

NOT ENOUGH: Yes, people do expect an ear each. The answer to this dilemma has two parts: the culinary and the psychological. The culinary: make a filling dish that goes with the main course. A bucket of biscuits with butter and honey will do nicely. How about lima beans with butter and brown sugar stirred in? The psychological: chop each ear of corn in half (in thirds if they're quite large) and pile them in a vegetable dish. Some people will take one, some two, some three or four. But no matter what, there will always be precisely one piece left when dinner is over. (Did you think we were going to suggest succotash? We don't think you need *that* much help.)

OLD, NOT SWEET: Any corn that has been thoughtfully prehusked for you by your well-meaning supermarket probably fits into this category.

Before you cook it, slice a small piece off the end and stand the ears, cut side down, in an inch of water for half an hour or so.

Whether or not you presoak the corn, try adding $1/2$ cup sugar to every 2 quarts of cooking water. A tablespoon or two of corn syrup will have the same beneficial effect.

OVERCOOKED: It is hard to imagine in our day and age, when you can buy frozen corn on the cob that tastes almost as good as mush on a stick, that someone in your family is going to bite into a steaming ear of fresh, sweet, hot-buttered corn and say, "Good grief, Zelda, you've overcooked the corn again."

If you feel guilty, however, give in and make the following recipe for fresh corn soup. The amount of work required will surely absolve you.

Fresh Corn Soup

FOR EACH CUP OF COOKED
   CORN KERNELS:
1 tablespoon butter
2 tablespoons chopped
   onion

1 tablespoon flour
1 cup milk
Salt, pepper, and nutmeg

Melt the butter in a heavy saucepan over medium heat. Add the
onion and flour, and cook for 3 minutes, stirring constantly. Warm the
milk in another pot (to avoid lumps later). Stir the corn into the onion
mixture and then add the milk. Warm the mixture thoroughly, but
do not boil. Season to taste with salt and pepper. Serve with a tiny
sprinkling of nutmeg.

SILKY: Corn silks can often be easily removed simply by holding the
ear under a hard stream of running water. The corn's ear, that is, of
course. Flick off the few remaining silks with a knife.

THAWED: Please see Appendix B for remarks on thawed corn that you
wish was still frozen.

TOO DARK: Some people think light-yellow corn tastes better than dark-
yellow corn. To fool such people, add a dash of vinegar to the water the
corn is boiling in, and the corn will turn at least a few shades lighter as
it cooks. There will, however, be no change in the taste.

TOO MUCH: Except in emergencies, corn on the cob should never be
reheated; it toughens the corn. Here is a simple yet interesting recipe
for leftover corn on the cob.

Delaware Corn Pudding

1 cup corn kernels
³/₄ cup bread crumbs
¹/₂ cup milk
1 egg yolk

¹/₂ green bell pepper, minced
Salt and pepper
1 egg white
2 slices uncooked bacon

In a baking dish, mix the corn with the bread crumbs, milk, egg yolk, bell pepper, and salt and pepper to taste. Beat the egg white until it holds stiff peaks and fold it into the corn mixture. Put the bacon slices on top and bake at 350°F for 30 minutes.

CORNED BEEF

BLAND: Once it's cooked, you'll just have to add a sauce with a little zip, or serve it with a good mustard (we're partial to stone-ground or perhaps a sweet and spicy). Next time, add any of the following four seasonings, alone or in concert, to the cooking water for corned beef or, indeed, for boiled beef: dill seed, a 1-inch stick of cinnamon, whole celery seed, or four or five whole allspice berries.

TOUGH: You haven't cooked it long enough. Just keep going. It takes a long, long while to get some corned beef tender, but it eventually does happen (unless you can detect the word "Firestone" stamped into the side of the beef).

CORNSTARCH

NEED SOME, HAVE NONE: For most cooking purposes, you can substitute 2 tablespoons regular flour for 1 tablespoon cornstarch. Or substitute equal amounts of potato starch, rice flour, or arrowroot. What we call cornstarch is actually called corn flour in England.

CORN SYRUP

NEED SOME, HAVE NONE: For 1 cup light corn syrup, substitute $1^1/_4$ cups sugar plus $^1/_4$ cup of liquid. For 1 cup dark corn syrup, substitute $^3/_4$ cup light corn syrup plus $^1/_4$ cup molasses or $1^1/_4$ cups dark brown sugar plus $^1/_4$ cup water.

CRAB: *see* FISH AND SEAFOOD

CRACKERS

NOT ENOUGH: Toast any kind of bread until dark (i.e., until the bread is brown, not until sunset). Using a knife with a serrated blade, saw the bread in half the hard way, making two full-sized thin slices instead of one regular one. Cut in quarters. Instant (nearly) crackers.

SOGGY: Put soggy crackers on a baking sheet and bake for 2 or 3 minutes at 350°F.

CRANBERRIES: *see* BERRIES

CREAM: *see also* MILK; SOUR CREAM; WHIPPED CREAM

NEED SOME, HAVE NONE: If you need sweet cream and have sour, baking soda sweetens sour cream. So add a pinch of soda to some sour cream and keep adding more, slowly, until the cream reaches the desired degree of sweetness. Start with a tiny, tiny pinch. A teaspoon per pint is the most you'd ever want to add, and rarely that much.

Or you can use powdered milk made with less water than usual, or by adding milk to the powder instead of water.

But why aren't you using your emergency can of evaporated milk? Just thought you might need a reminder—you did set those emergency supplies aside, didn't you? For whipped cream, refrigerate both the milk and your beaters and then whip. Add sugar as desired. A word of warning, though: this works best served on cold desserts. If you put your nicely whipped evaporated milk on, say, a slice of warm pie, it will rapidly revert to its liquid state. You can also just slightly dilute the milk as a substitute for cream.

SOUR: Bet you can guess if you've read the rest of the section: a pinch of baking soda will sweeten sour cream.

CREAM PUFFS

BEADS OF MOISTURE: This happens when cream puffs are underbaked. Return them to the hot oven, turn off the oven at once, and let them sit in there for 5 minutes with the door slightly ajar (the traditional oven door prop is a wooden spoon). The beads of moisture should disappear.

COLLAPSED AND SOGGY: Cream puffs collapse when they are cooked on the outside and too moist on the inside. So slice off the top, remove the moist dough with your fingers (yes, you can eat it), replace the top, and return to the hot oven. Turn off the oven, leave the door ajar, and wait for 10 minutes. Then proceed normally.

Next time, here's the professionals' method for perfect puffs: as soon as they're cooled, put your puffs in the freezer. Even if you're serving them the same day, freeze them. When you're ready to assemble them, put them on a baking sheet in a 350°F oven for 2 minutes. Slice them in half and fill. They'll be crisp outside and soft inside, just as they should be.

DIDN'T PUFF: Make a splendid dish with crispy outsides by coating the unpuffed puffs with caramelized sugar. Toss them (using two forks) in a pot of caramelized sugar. Let them harden (which happens almost instantly) and then split them and fill as you had planned.

CREAM SOUP: *see* SOUPS

CRÈME FRAÎCHE

NEED SOME, HAVE NONE: For many purposes, you can use sour cream in equal amounts. Crème fraîche is milder, however, so you may want to add some cream to lessen the sourness. Of course, it will now be thinner (but you knew that). If it is in a recipe that will be cooked, use gentle heat because sour cream breaks down when heated and crème fraîche doesn't.

If you have the time, you can just make your own using the following recipe. Here's an excerpt from a book called *Café Beaujolais* (by Margaret Fox and John Bear, Ten Speed Press, 1984): "[Crème fraîche] has a mellower flavor than sour cream—sort of nutty, instead of tangy. I love it, and use it in place of sour cream all the time. You can whip it and make it thicker, the same way you do with cream, or you can use it in the more liquid state."

Crème Fraîche

Heavy cream
Buttermilk

Combine the cream with the buttermilk (1 tablespoon for each cup of cream) in a saucepan over medium heat. Heat just until the chill is off—to about 50°F. Pour into a glass jar, cover lightly with a piece of waxed paper, and let sit in a warm place (65°F to 70°F) for 12 to 20 hours, until the crème fraîche has thickened. Replace the waxed paper with plastic wrap or a tight-fitting lid and refrigerate for at least 6 hours before using. It keeps for up to 2 weeks.

CREPES

TEAR WHEN FLIPPED: Cook them a bit longer or up the heat a little. Some of us swear by a nonstick pan, but for those who consider such a thing sacrilege, make sure your pan is properly seasoned and greased.

CRISCO: *see* FAT, LARD, SHORTENING

CROQUETTES

WON'T FIRM UP: There are few things worse than a flabby croquette. To fix this problem, soak 1 teaspoon gelatin in 2 tablespoons cold water and then dissolve it over boiling water. Stir it into the croquette mixture and wait until the gelatin hardens. The heat of cooking will dissolve the gelatin, and the croquette will be soft and creamy inside.

CUCUMBERS

BLAND: Maybe what they need is dill seed. Try sprinkling some on sliced or marinated cucumbers or in a cucumber salad. Or maybe try celery seed.

SOGGY, WILTED: Put the cucumbers, whole, in a basin of cold water in the refrigerator. About an hour before you want to eat the cucumbers, peel and slice them, sprinkle them with salt, and put them back in the water. Drain before serving. As an alternative, you can make this soup.

Bulgarian Cucumber Soup

Plain yogurt
Cucumbers
A few pinches of sugar

A few pinches of fresh or
dried dill weed
Salt and pepper

Mix together 1 cup yogurt for every ¹/₂ to 1 cup cucumbers. Add the sugar and dill and season to taste with salt and pepper.

TOO MANY: If the cucumbers are nice, firm, unshriveled, and dark green, they will keep for at least a week. If they are losing their freshness, you'd better hurry up and make something. There's nothing that tastes more summery than a gazpacho. Most basic cookbooks will have a recipe. If that isn't interesting enough for you, how about this Indonesian condiment? It goes well with curries or simple grilled meat (or tofu or tempeh).

Sambal

1 cup ¹/₄-inch chunks fresh
pineapple
1 cup ¹/₄-inch chunks seeded
cucumber
2 teaspoons sugar

1 large shallot, finely chopped
1 tablespoon soy sauce
1 tablespoon lime juice
Salt

Combine all of the ingredients in a bowl. Cover and chill for 1 hour.

Another solution for excess cucumbers is to slice them fairly thick—¹/₂ inch or so—bread them, if you wish, and sauté them until brown. Turn the cucumbers over and brown the other side. You could do the same with green tomatoes and wow your friends and family with a "hot salad." Or do the obvious and make pickles. It's simpler than you think. Consult a basic cookbook.

More cucumbers? Try this interesting salad.

Swedish Pressed Cucumber Salad

2 cucumbers, peeled and very thinly sliced	3 tablespoons white vinegar
	2 tablespoons sugar
2 teaspoons salt	Freshly ground pepper

Place the cucumber slices in a colander and sprinkle with the salt. Cover with a plate and place something heavy on top to press them (a large can works well). Chill for 1 hour. Pour off the juices and put the cucumbers in a bowl. Combine the vinegar and sugar and pour over the top. Add pepper to taste. Chill for 1 hour.

CUPCAKES: *see* CAKES

CURRY POWDER: *see also* HERBS, SPICES

TOO MUCH: If you can't or don't want to dilute the effect with more of the basic ingredient of the dish, you have two options: serve with more rice or add things to the curry. If you serve the dish with lots of rice, then the curried item becomes almost a flavoring agent. Things to serve with and add to the curry that provide a respite from the spiciness are chopped cucumber (plain or combined with plain yogurt), chopped banana, yogurt with chopped mild vegetables in it, chopped orange or mandarin orange segments (canned is all right), or canned lychees.

CUSTARDS: *see* PUDDINGS AND CUSTARDS

DAIKON

BITTER: Daikon is usually milder than your common red radish. If yours is still too bitter, it's said that cooking it in water in which rice has been rinsed or to which a bit of rice has been added will eliminate some of the bitterness. If you're planning to serve it raw, just slice it very thin and perhaps serve with a rich dip.

LIMP: Soak in ice water until recrisped. (If you soak thin slices, however, they will curl up like potato chips. In case you were wondering.)

DATES

STUCK TO EACH OTHER: Put them in a warm oven for a few minutes and they should unstick. If you're going to add them to muffins, bread, or other baked goods, toss the diced dates with the dry ingredients so each piece is coated with flour. This will make them less likely to sink in clumps.

STUCK TO UTENSIL: Next time, dip the utensil (scissors or a knife, presumably) in cold water, and cut the dates while the utensil is still wet.

DOUGHNUTS

OILY: Pat them with a paper towel to remove the grease. With the rest of the batch, let the cut-out dough air-dry for 15 minutes before frying. They will develop a slight crust, which will reduce the amount of fat they absorb. Also, make sure you don't fry too many at once. This brings down the oil temperature, and cool oil means greasy doughnuts.

DRINKS, ALCOHOLIC: *see* ALCOHOL

DUCK: *see* POULTRY

DUMPLINGS

FALLING APART IN POT: If they're just starting to fall apart, try turning down the heat under them. A steady simmer is what you're aiming for. Boiling can cause dumpling disintegration. If it's already too late, rescue the bits from the pot (you may have to scrape some from the bottom) and transfer them to a paper towel–lined colander. Press them to make dry bits. Pile in a buttered dish, cover loosely with foil, and bake for 20 minutes at 350°F. Serve them as baked dumplings, perhaps with a flavorful sauce.

HEAVY: Did you peek? Next time, let the dumplings cook undisturbed. Drafts of air will deflate some dumplings. If you can't stand the suspense, invest in a pot with a glass lid.

DURIAN

STINKY: Yes, they are stinky. Some people love them. Others don't. Those who love them usually don't mind the smell. If you mind it, perhaps you should give the fruit to someone who doesn't.

EGGS, GENERAL: *see also* EGGS, BOILED; EGGS, DEVILED; EGGS, FRIED; EGGS, POACHED; EGGS, SCRAMBLED; EGG WHITES; EGG YOLKS; OMELETTES

COLD: Eggs should be at room temperature for baking. To bring an egg from refrigerator temperature to room temperature quickly, without cooking it in the process, dunk it in lukewarm water for 5 minutes.

DROPPED ON THE FLOOR: Cover the mess with a lot of salt. Then cover the salt with a bowl or pot, so the dog doesn't get into it and nobody walks through it, tracking salt and egg all over the house. In 20 minutes, the whole mess should sweep up easily with a broom and dustpan. (Does anybody have a recipe calling for egg-flavored salt?)

EGGSHELL IN EGG: Probably the simplest way to remove bits of eggshell from eggs is to use an empty eggshell half as a scoop.

NOT ENOUGH: In baking, you can generally replace about one egg in three with a tablespoon of cornstarch. Other possible substitutes for one egg in baking include: 1 tablespoon ground flax seed mixed with 3 tablespoons water (works great in whole-grain items); ¼ cup silken tofu (best in dense cakes and brownies); and half a mashed banana (good in muffins, quick breads, and pancakes).

OVERCOOKED: Overcooked fried, poached, scrambled, and other such eggs tend to be tough. So why not continue cooking them until they are totally overcooked, and then use them instead of hard-boiled eggs in salads, sandwiches, and the like?

However, if your problem is that the breakfast eggs have overcooked and everyone is sitting there clamoring for breakfast, there is still hope.

Quick Chilaquiles

FOR EVERY FOUR EGGS:
2 to 3 cups gently crushed
  tortilla chips
2 cups enchilada sauce, a mix
  of salsa and tomato sauce,
  or plain red or green salsa

1 cup shredded cheddar
  cheese
Sour cream (optional)
Avocado (optional)

Put the chips into a frying pan over medium heat. Pour the sauce over and cover the pan. Simmer until the chips have absorbed some of the sauce and softened, about 5 minutes. Sprinkle the cheese over the top and cover again for a minute or two, just until the cheese is melted. Scoop out with a spatula onto your eggs. Serve with tortillas if you have some. In fact, if you don't have any tortilla chips, you can use tortillas instead. Cut them into strips and fry them in oil until brown before adding the sauce. Top with sour cream if you have it. Or avocado.

STUCK TO CARTON: Wet the carton and the eggs will come out without cracking.

STUCK TO EGG BEATER, POTS, ETC.: The secret to cleaning up eggs is to use cold water, not hot.

TOO MUCH FAT IN THEM: There's not much you can do to remove the fat from egg yolks, but you can often use just the whites alone, or mostly whites and a small amount of yolk, in recipes calling for whole eggs. Feed the yolks to your pets, if that's something they can eat, or just consider them the "pits" of the egg and toss them. Sure, it's extravagant, but hospitalization for a coronary is even more expensive!

UNCERTAIN QUALITY: Test for freshness by lowering raw eggs into water. If they float, that means there are air pockets under the shell and they are old.

YOLK IN THE WHITE: When you separate the eggs and there are bits of yolk in the white, it is important to remove them, because the whites may not whip unless you do. Remove the yolk with a yolk magnet, which consists of a cloth moistened in cold water. Touch it to the yolk and it will cling.

EGGS, BOILED: *see also various other* EGG *categories*

CRACKED BEFORE COOKING: Wrap the egg very tightly in aluminum foil, twisting the ends. Then boil it normally. After boiling the egg, plunge it quickly into cold water. If you don't, it will continue to cook in the foil.

CRACKED DURING COOKING: Pour in 1 teaspoon salt. It should keep the whites from seeping out. A few drops of lemon juice or vinegar in the egg water will have the same effect.

CRUMBLY, DIFFICULT TO SLICE: If you don't have an egg-slicing gadget, the easiest way to slice hard-boiled eggs is either to use a cheese slicer or to garrote the eggs with thread. Or you can use a hot dry knife.

DIFFICULT TO PEEL: Tap all over the shell of the warm cooked egg with a spoon, and/or roll the egg around in cold water. Peel it under gently running water. If you have a pot full of hard-boiled eggs, just pour most of the water off and shake the pot to crack the eggs against each other. Add cold water to cool the eggs and then peel them.

DISCOLORED: Dark circles around the yolks of freshly hard-boiled eggs can be prevented by cooking the eggs properly. Cover eggs with cool water to a height of 1 inch above the tops of the eggs and bring them rapidly to a boil. Take the pan off the heat, cover, and let stand for 20 minutes. Cool immediately in cold water.

If the eggs already have dark yolks, hold each yolk under a gentle stream of cold water and lightly rub it with your finger.

OFF-CENTER YOLKS: You can't change them now, but next time roll each raw egg a couple of feet horizontally (always in the same direction) before you put it in the hot water.

TOO MANY: Peeled hard-boiled eggs can be stored in the refrigerator, covered by water, for 2 or 3 days. Frankly, "too many" is a great excuse for egg salad or deviled eggs (see more hints below under "EGGS, DEVILED").

UNDERCOOKED: If you have opened a soft- or medium-boiled egg in the "proper" fashion, by cutting off just a bit of the narrow end, you can cook it more by lowering it back into boiling water, suspended in cloth or cheesecloth. Don't let the water enter the egg. Alternatively, enclose your egg in a piece of foil that's big enough so you can gather the edges on top, over the opened end. Support it, vertically, in your pot between something a few minutes of boiling water won't injure (coffee mugs? rocks?). If this method won't work, convert your boiled egg to a scrambled or, possibly, fried egg.

EGGS, DEVILED: *see also various other* EGG *categories*

BLAND: Try adding crushed basil, cumin, curry, tarragon, and/or thyme to make deviled eggs a bit more devilish. A drop of Tabasco sauce makes for a lively mix. Dust with paprika or chile powder for a fancy-looking treat.

EGGS, FRIED: *see also various other* EGG *categories*

GREASE SPLATTERING: Sprinkle salt on the pan or griddle prior to heating it. This will impart a nice flavor to the eggs, as well.

OVERCOOKED: See "EGGS, GENERAL, Overcooked."

EGGS, POACHED: *see also various other* EGG *categories*

OVERCOOKED: See "EGGS, GENERAL, Overcooked."

MESSY-LOOKING: A few drops of vinegar in the water will help keep egg yolks from floating all over the pot while you're poaching eggs.

A famous egg chef (thank you, Mary Ann G.) taught us that if you make a little whirlpool or vortex in the water using a spoon, and you drop the raw egg right into the center of the vortex, it will all stay together instead of floating around the pot.

EGGS, SCRAMBLED: *see also various other* EGG *categories*

BLAND: In addition to all the usual stuff, like onions and mushrooms and tomatoes and spinach, consider the following seasonings, all of which are compatible with scrambled eggs: basil, chervil, ground cloves, cumin, curry, marjoram, toasted poppy seeds, rosemary, tarragon, thyme, and turmeric. Or try grating in a bit of Parmesan cheese for a rich taste in exchange for a few extra calories.

OVERCOOKED: 1) Chop up to use on salads, for garnishes, in fried rice, or in egg salad. See also "EGGS, GENERAL, Overcooked." 2) Put on toast, sprinkle with shredded cheese, and run under the broiler until the cheese melts.

TOUGH: Salt tends to make cooked eggs tough. Next time, add the salt after cooking. (Pepper doesn't have this effect.)

EGG WHITES: *see also* EGGS, GENERAL

NOT ENOUGH: Before beating, add 1 teaspoon cream of tartar for each cup of egg whites. They will beat up fluffier, thus having greater volume.

OVERWHIPPED: If you've overwhipped your egg whites, they've lost some of the volume you were going for. It is possible that adding an extra egg white and whipping again, carefully this time, will rescue your whites. If you get a nice volume, you can continue with your recipe as planned. You don't need to change any recipe proportions. However, this fix doesn't always work. You may need to start over with fresh egg whites.

TOO MANY: Freeze them, one to an ice cube tray section. When they are frozen, remove them from the tray and store them in a plastic bag in the freezer. They will last for months.

WON'T WHIP: The eggs should be at least 3 days old. If you got them at a supermarket, they probably are. They should also be at room temperature. Either let them sit for 30 minutes or dunk them in lukewarm water for 5 minutes.

The beaters must be very clean and free of grease; even a tiny bit may retard whipping.

And if you've done all that and they still won't whip, add a pinch of cream of tartar or a few drops of lemon juice. The whites may be a bit fluffier than usual, but they will whip.

EGG YOLKS

LEFTOVER: If the yolks are unbroken, cover them with water or milk. They will last for 2 or 3 days in the refrigerator. If broken, or unbroken but more than 2 or 3 days old, freeze them. Stabilize them with a tiny pinch of salt or sugar (depending on your probable future use of them) for each yolk. Consider freezing them separately, perhaps in an ice cube tray, for future use one at a time.

Those of us lowering our fat intake tend to accumulate egg yolks. They are still good food and unparalleled for making a pastry crust that's rich-looking and shiny without adding too much fat. If you've many accumulated yolks, do you have a dog or cat? An egg yolk every few days is good for the coat. Or you can beat an egg yolk into a few tablespoons of your shampoo (just before using, please). Some people swear it "feeds" the hair without going through the digestive tract. Hmm.

EGGPLANTS

BITTER: The peel can be the bitter part. So, one way or another, try to remove it. One way: See "Difficult to Peel," this section. Another: Using a 12-gauge shotgun. Oh, never mind.

If removing the peel isn't feasible (the eggplant is already in pieces in a stew or something), keep cooking it. Lengthy cooking can make eggplant less bitter. Older eggplants tend to be more bitter, so use them fairly quickly. The best way to avoid bitterness, however, is to start your recipe by cutting the raw eggplant into slices and sprinkling it with salt. Let the slices sit for 30 to 60 minutes and then blot with a paper towel.

BLAND: There are those who feel that the best way to improve an eggplant is to encase it in cement and drop it in the river. For those who disagree with this sentiment, here are some seasonings that will improve the flavor of a bland eggplant: basil, celery seed, chervil, oregano, sage, and thyme. If you're breading the eggplant, put the herbs in the breading. If you're frying it, sprinkle the herbs on before cooking.

DIFFICULT TO PEEL: Try to remove the skin from slices of eggplant by cutting with a pair of scissors. If you want to end up with mashed eggplant, however, consider charring the skin. Hold the eggplant over an open flame (the gas range works fine for this), skewered on a big fork, until the skin is blackened all over. This takes a while, so arm yourself with a good paperback book to read. When it looks done, put it in a small paper bag and let it sit for 15 minutes. Then rub off the skin under cold running water. If it needs further cooking, you can steam it or bake it or slice and sauté it. The smoky flavor is in the flesh and won't wash away.

DISCOLORED: If a slice should start to discolor, drop it in salt water to retard the discoloration.

GREASY: Eggplants are grease sponges. The only thing to do once it is oily is to blot off as much of the grease as you can with a paper towel. If some of your eggplant is still raw, try the salt trick on the rest (see "Bitter," above). Salting eggplant draws out the water and makes it denser, which it turn tends to make it soak up less oil during cooking. Breading your eggplant is another way to reduce oil absorption.

FALAFEL

FALLS APART DURING COOKING: There may be too much moisture in the falafel mixture. Add a bit of flour to the remaining mixture—but not too much, or your falafel will be dry. Cook one and see if it holds together. Also, make sure your oil is hot enough for frying—350°F is a good temperature.

FAT, LARD, SHORTENING

DIFFICULT TO GET OUT OF CAN: When shortening or other solid fats get down toward the bottom of the can, fill the can with boiling water, let it cool, and the shortening will float to the top, enabling you to utilize it down (up?) to the last drop.

SMELLY: To remove odors from frying fat that you'd like to reuse, fry potato slices in it until they are brown. The potato will sop up all the extraneous odors, even powerful ones like fish and onion. Why not do the potatoes last, then, and have a fish-and-chips dinner?

FENNEL

FLAVOR TOO STRONG: Cook it. (Or cook it longer.) This mutes the intensity of the licorice flavor.

FLAVOR TOO WEAK: Chop some fennel fronds and add them to your dish at the end of cooking.

FIGS

BLAND: Try powdered cinnamon, or you can stir ¹/₄ teaspoon powdered cardamom into ¹/₂ cup honey and spoon it over the figs. Also try adding ¹/₄ teaspoon dried rosemary to ¹/₄ cup boiling water. Remove it from the heat and let steep until the water is cool. Strain out the rosemary and pour the water over the figs.

STUCK TOGETHER: When dried figs stick together, heat the whole shebang in the oven at 300°F for a few minutes.

FISH AND SEAFOOD

BLAND: Just about any herb or spice you have in the house can be used in some fashion on most fish dishes. Go wild. To help you get started thinking about this, here is a partial list of useful seasonings:

allspice (four or five whole berries in the cooking water)
anise (good with cod)

basil (for broiled or scalloped fish)
bay leaf
chervil
cinnamon (try it in bouillon, but start with just a little)
coriander (on baked or broiled fish)
curry
dill weed
fennel
garlic
ginger (on broiled fish, use ground or grated fresh ginger)
mace (with trout)
marjoram (on broiled, baked, or creamed fish)
mustard (on fried or baked fish)
nutmeg
oregano
paprika
rosemary (on salmon)
saffron (in sauces)
savory
sesame seed (on fried, broiled, or baked fish)
tarragon (on lobster, tuna, or salmon)

BREADING FALLS OFF: See "BREADING, Falls Off."

DRY: Serve with a sauce or simply melted butter and silvered almonds.

CANNED FLAVOR: To make canned seafood like crab, tuna, or salmon taste uncanny, soak it in fresh whatever-liquid-it-was-packed-in (either oil or water) for about half an hour.

CAN'T FIND THE KIND YOU NEED: Sometimes a recipe calls for a particular type of fish but it isn't available in the store where you shop. Or maybe you don't want to use it because overfishing has made it an ecologically unsound choice. If you are concerned about making eco-friendly choices, we recommend you check out the website of either the Environmental Defense Fund (www.edf.org) or the Monterey Aquarium (www.montereybayaquarium.org), both of which have pages on sustainable seafood recommendations.

Otherwise, here are several categories of fish; within each category, the different types of fish are more or less interchangeable.

Lean firm fish: grouper, mahi-mahi, marlin, monkfish, shark, swordfish, tilapia

Fatty firm fish: catfish, eel, sturgeon, tuna

Lean flaky fish: cod, flounder, hake, sand dab, sole

Fatty flaky fish: herring, salmon, sardine, trout

FISHY FLAVOR: Some fish taste too, well, fishy for some people. A sauce involving brandy, sherry, or ginger lessens the fishiness.

Boiled fish sometimes tastes too fishy. Let it stand in the cooking water or sauce after it is cooked and the flavor will dissipate somewhat.

OVERCOOKED: "When you overcook a fish," someone's grandmother must have said, "boil the hell out of it and make fish stock." Check your cookbooks for all the wondrous things to do with fish stock, among which is the following.

Sauce Velouté

2 tablespoons butter
2 tablespoons flour
1 cup fish stock

Capers, mashed anchovies, or mashed sardines (optional)

Melt the butter in a saucepan over medium heat. Whisk in the flour and cook, whisking, until the mixture is smooth and beginning to brown. Whisk in the fish stock, bring to a simmer, and simmer, stirring until thickened. Add optional ingredients as you please. You can pour the sauce directly onto any fish, right there on the plate, or you can create a casserole by pouring the sauce over some bland cooked fish. Add boiled sliced potatoes, if you wish, and heat at 350°F for 20 minutes.

If you have the time, overcooked fish can also be made into fish cakes or croquettes. The binding sauce will restore some of the moisture.

SCALY: If an allegedly scaled fish still has scales on it, and you don't feel like hiking back to the fish seller to trade it in, try plunging the fish into scalding water, then into cold water, and then scraping off the now-loosened scales with a serrated knife such as a grapefruit knife.

SHELLFISH, DIFFICULT TO SHELL: Next time, cook shrimp, crayfish, or other shellfish in water to which you have added 1 tablespoon white wine vinegar for each quart of water. The flesh will be firmer without overcooking, and you will find the shells easier to remove. This time, try peeling them under warm running water, letting the water help detach the shells.

SMELLY: When you're frying fish, the more dreadful smells usually come from the hot fat, not from the fish itself. Reduce the heat and see if that doesn't help.

When poaching fish, add some celery leaves to the pot. They will help minimize the fish smell (not entirely, however; who wants a fish that smells like celery?), and they smell pretty good themselves.

In general, a caramel type of odor tends to neutralize fishy odors. So either issue caramels to your guests, or cook some granulated sugar in a pan. Either use a disposable pan, or line a regular saucepan with aluminum foil to avoid a messy clean-up job. Or perhaps you could plan a caramel sauce over ice cream for dessert?

TOO MUCH: If it's already cooked, make timbales, croquettes, fish cakes, or even (for firm-fleshed fish) a salad.

FLAMBÉED DISHES: *see* ALCOHOL, Brandy or Liqueur Won't Ignite

FLOUR, ALL-PURPOSE

NEED SOME, HAVE NONE: For 1 cup of all-purpose flour, you can substitute 1 cup plus 2 tablespoons cake flour. In many baking situations, 1 1/2 cups rolled oats can replace 1 cup all-purpose flour. Consider whirling your oatmeal in the food processor to make the texture finer if you try this. If the flour is a thickener in your recipe, substitute half as much cornstarch or arrowroot.

FLOUR, SELF-RISING

NEED SOME, HAVE NONE: For each cup, use 1 cup all-purpose flour plus 1^1/$_2$ teaspoons baking powder and ^{1}/$_2$ teaspoon salt.

FONDUE

CHEESE, STRINGY: Stringiness may be caused by overheating or over-stirring. You may be able to rescue the cheese with a splash of white wine or lemon juice gently stirred in. Adding a bit of cornstarch may also help. If it becomes too thick, keep adding wine. Adding more cheese may work, too. If nothing works, enjoy it anyway. There are few things more fun than sharing stringy fondue with friends. Hilarity will ensue.

CHOCOLATE, SEPARATED: Chocolate fondue needs to be kept at a very low heat. Try adding a bit of cream, but accept that it may be too late.

FOWL: *see* POULTRY

FRANKFURTERS: *see* SAUSAGES

FRENCH FRIES

SOGGY: Some us actually prefer soggy, dense French fries. The rest of you, however, should use starchy potatoes (like russets), soak them in ice water for an hour or so after cutting them, make sure your oil is hot enough, and don't overcrowd your pot. Some people swear by the double-fry method. Fry your french fries for the first time for about 2 minutes in oil at 330°F to 360°F (until cooked but still white), and then let cool for at least 10 minutes. Fry for a second time at 365°F to 375°F until golden and crisp. We've heard of people triple cooking them (by boiling them first before double frying them), but that's just beyond the pale. Whatever your method, serve french fries immediately after cooking. Trying to keep them warm is bound to make them limp.

FRITTATA

BOTTOM IS DONE, TOP IS RUNNY: Covering your pan while cooking will take care of this problem. For now, run it under the broiler (but keep an eye on it, because it will cook in just a minute or so).

FROSTING: *see* ICING

FROZEN FOODS: *see specific foods; also* APPENDIX B

FRUITS: *see specific fruit*

FRUITCAKE: *see also* CAKES

OLD AND DRY: Cut deep slits in the top and pour in brandy or sherry to taste. Wrap the cake in plastic and let it stand overnight to let it all sink in. Please do not drive after eating.

FUDGE: *see* CANDY

GAME

GAME BIRDS, TOUGH: Often the breast is the only part of a game bird that isn't tough. Serve that and save the rest to make stock. If that means you don't have enough bird, see "POULTRY, Not Enough."

TOO GAMY: Well, it is game after all. Just try to embrace the gaminess. Or whip up a sauce made with lots of wine, shallots, mustard, and butter to cover up the flavor of the meat. Next time, try marinating before cooking, soak the meat in saltwater overnight (as some very old cookbooks suggest), or just stick with the supermarket meat selection.

TOUGH OR DRY: Game meat contains less fat than farm-raised meat, so it dries out more quickly. The tougher parts, like the shoulder and leg cuts, are best braised until tender. The lean loin cuts are at their peak grilled, seared, or roasted not a hair past medium to preserve the little moisture they have. If you've already overcooked it, there's not much to be done except smother it with gravy or jus. You can also try chopping it very small and covering it with a sauce. But taste it first. I've had buffalo chewing gum and nothing could save it (though it did have a nice flavor).

GARLIC

DIFFICULT TO PEEL: Here are five things to try: 1) If the peel is slightly loose, run hot water over the garlic and the peel should come off readily. 2) Cut off the root end of the garlic cloves (the flattish end at the bottom of the bulb). Mash them with the side of a big kitchen knife. The peel should be easy to separate from the clove. 3) If you need whole cloves and you've got a little time, drop the garlic into boiling water for 5 seconds, then drop it into cold water. The peel should now come off easily. 4) Microwave the cloves on high for 10 to 20 seconds, then rub gently.

NEED SOME, HAVE NONE: You can substitute garlic powder, though it will have a slightly different taste. Taste as you go, but plan on about $^1/_2$ teaspoon per clove.

GELATIN

STUCK IN MOLD: Loosen the gelatin around the edges with the tip of a knife. Dip the mold in hot water (not so far that the water runs onto the gelatin) for a few seconds, invert it onto a plate, and shake the mold off slowly. If it is still stuck, repeat. If it is *still* stuck, give up. Perhaps you used library paste instead of gelatin powder. (Next time, lightly oil the mold before adding the gelatin.)

TIME IS SHORT: If you don't even have time to follow the "quick method" given on most boxes, try this "even quicker" method, which may be up to 50 percent faster. Add just enough hot water to the powder to dissolve it. A few tablespoons should be enough. Then use ice water for the rest of the liquid. If you add fruits, they should be very cold.

TOO THICK: If you let your gelatin set too long and you wanted to stir in fruits or marbles or something and now you can't, warm it up by any convenient means (the oven, stove, or setting it in a bowl of warm water) and it will thinnen (which is the opposite of thicken). Then let it set again to the right consistency for stirring stuff in.

TOO THIN: If a gelatin dessert or salad won't thicken at all, or it isn't setting fast enough for you, set it in an ice bath. An ice bath is a big bowl full of ice cubes and water. Next time, be sure you let the gelatin soak in cold liquid for 5 minutes before using it.

GLUTEN-FREE BAKED GOODS

TOUGH, DENSE, CRUMBLY, RUBBERY: Gluten is a protein found in grains. It gives dough elasticity (so it rises) and strength (so it doesn't crumble). But many people are allergic to gluten. Gluten-free baking is possible, but it takes a bit of effort to find gluten-free flours (which include rice, chickpea, and potato flours) and to learn to use them properly. Different flours have different properties that will affect the taste and texture of your baked goods, so we don't recommend a wholesale replacement of gluten-free flour for all-purpose flour unless you've bought a gluten-free baking mix made just for that purpose. Otherwise, you would be best served by consulting a gluten-free cookbook.

GOOSEBERRIES: *see* BERRIES

GOULASH: *see* STEWS

GRAPEFRUITS

DIFFICULT TO GET THE PITH OFF: When you've peeled a grapefruit and there is still a lot of the white pith on it, you can either scrape at the pith with the edge of your serrated grapefruit knife, or you can dunk the grapefruit in hot water for 2 minutes. Next time, boil the grapefruit for 5 minutes before peeling and all the pith will come away with the peel.

DIFFICULT TO PEEL: Pour boiling water over the grapefruit and let it stand for 5 minutes in the water. It should then peel readily. You can dunk it in cold water if it's too hot to handle. The peel won't reattach, we promise.

NOT JUICY: If there are two of you (people, not grapefruits), stand at opposite ends of the room and roll the grapefruit back and forth for a few minutes. Rolling it around on a tabletop in a circular motion (like making balls out of clay) will have the same effect, although it is not nearly as much fun. Another option is to cook the grapefruit in a microwave oven, at medium heat, for 15 seconds.

SOUR: Curiously enough, a bit of salt has the effect of making sour grapefruit taste sweeter.

GRAPES

TOO SOUR (OR TOO MANY): Some people mix up a fruit salad with a sweet dressing (some even use marshmallow creme!). But we find that the sourness of the grapes may still sneak through. Making jelly is a good way to use up sour grapes since you can add as much sugar as you want. There's another option as well. In the early fall, we find ourselves swimming in the grapes that grow on our arbor. They aren't great eating grapes because they are so sour, but every year we make large batches of this sorbet.

Grape Sorbet

1/3 cup sugar
1/3 cup plus 1/4 cup water
1 1/2 pounds red grapes,
   preferably Concord

1 1/2 tablespoons lemon juice

In a small saucepan over low heat, combine the sugar and 1/3 cup water and cook, stirring, until the sugar dissolves. Set aside to cool. Combine the grapes and the remaining 1/4 cup water in a medium saucepan over medium-high heat. Cook until the grapes start releasing their liquid. Reduce the heat to medium and simmer until the grapes break apart, about 3 minutes. Pass the mixture through a food mill or a fine sieve. Let cool. Stir in the lemon juice followed by the sugar syrup until sweetened to your liking. Refrigerate until cold. Transfer the mixture to an ice-cream maker and freeze according to the manufacturer's instructions.

GRAVY

BLAND, FLAT, PALLID, GRAY: Depending on the kind of gravy, consider adding any of the following five types of ingredients:

1. Herbs and spices; for instance, ground allspice, coriander, marjoram, mustard, savory, or thyme.

2. Extracts, such as bouillon cubes, yeast extracts, or meat extracts.

3. Alcohol, of which sherry and port are most traditional, but white vermouth is an interesting variation.

4. Bottled seasonings, such as soy sauce, Tabasco, Worcester-shire, A.1. Steak Sauce, and so on.

5. Red currant jelly.

FATTY: If the fat is mostly on the top, you can either skim it off or sop it up with a piece of bread. If you're being fanatical, let it stand. While the fat is floating up to the top, tear paper towels into wide strips. Float these on top, one at a time, drawing them off toward the edge. They'll remove the last traces of fat. If the fat is in the middle (and isn't that the case with most of us?), the easiest thing to do is to chill the gravy (quickly, in the freezer, if necessary), skim the fat off, and reheat it. Next time, you may wish to get one of those clever gravy boats, in which the spout goes to the bottom, so you are pouring from the lean bottom of the gravy rather than the fatty top.

LUMPY: Beat lumpy gravy with a whisk or with a hand-operated rotary beater. Use a blender or food processor only as a last resort. Or pour (or force) the gravy through a mesh strainer. Delumping gravy may make it too thin, in which case see "Too Thin," below.

NOT BROWN ENOUGH: To darken gravy quickly without affecting the flavor, add 1 teaspoon instant coffee.

NOT ENOUGH: If there aren't enough drippings left in the pan to make any gravy at all, add 1 cup water and a bouillon cube to whatever is in the pan, and cook until the cube is dissolved.

If you have some gravy but not enough, either add one of the many kinds of canned gravy available, or try this very fast substitute: to every ¹/₂ cup of gravy, add 1 teaspoon meat-flavoring sauce (e.g., Worcestershire or steak sauce), 1 teaspoon lemon juice, and one 8-ounce can tomato sauce.

SALTY: The only certain way to decrease saltiness is to increase the quantity of the gravy. A few pinches of brown sugar often have the effect of overcoming saltiness without adding noticeable sweetness. Or, for minor oversalting, cut a raw potato into thin slices and cook them in the gravy until they become translucent, then remove the slices.

TOO THIN: The best thickening agent is time. (Not thyme, time.) As a gravy cooks, the water evaporates, so it becomes thicker. If you don't have time, or you can't afford to reduce the quantity, here are the most common thickening agents:

1. Arrowroot. Use about 1 tablespoon per cup of liquid, dissolved in cold water and then stirred in within 10 minutes of serving.

2. Cornstarch. Use about 1 tablespoon per cup of liquid dissolved in cold water, then add the mixture to the gravy. To remove the constarchy taste and allow the gravy to thicken, bring it to a boil.

3. A roux. This is the favorite method of many pros. For 1 cup of liquid to be thickened, melt 1 to 2 tablespoons butter in a small pan, add an equal amount of flour to form a thick paste, and cook it a bit. Then whisk the roux into the gravy and bring it to a full boil to get it to thicken.

Other thickeners for various situations are rice, barley, a paste of flour and water (also good for scrapbooks and papier-mâché), milk, cream, egg yolks (remember the ones you put in the freezer?), mashed potato flakes, and (ugh) blood (preferably that of a bird or animal, not the chef, added just before serving). Here comes the most helpful suggestion on this page: never boil blood! (It will separate into protein solids and liquid.)

GREEN BEANS: *see* BEANS, LIMA AND GREEN

GREEN ONIONS: *see* ONIONS

GREENS

ARUGULA, TOO BITTER: Well, it's supposed to be a bitter green, but some arugula is more bitter than others, and the bitterness does intensify as it ages. If you're using it raw (we assume in a salad), tear it up really small and mix with other, blander, greens. If you're cooking it, you can mix it with a less bitter green (like spinach), or it is complemented nicely by white beans.

BLAND: For cooked greens, try adding one or more of these: mace, marjoram, or rosemary to the cooking water; a sprinkling of poppy seeds or sesame seeds on the finished product. Do you like vinegar? Balsamic vinegar sprinkled on hot greens is tasty! A squeeze of lemon juice and a bit of garlic (fresh or powdered) can be nice, too.

For raw greens, add anise (about 1/4 teaspoon, crushed, per 4 servings), basil, chervil, caraway, or savory.

BROWNING: If your lettuce or other greens are looking brown or rusty, store them in a plastic bag along with a couple of paper napkins to absorb the excess moisture, which is the problem. Some supermarkets drench their greens. They look dewy, but they rot in a few days when you bring them home. Drain such greens well before refrigerating with those paper towels.

COLLARDS, TOUGH: Collards tend to be more fibrous, and thus tougher, than other greens. Cut out the middle stem and cook them longer than other greens. Some recipes will have you cook them all day, but really about 30 minutes ought to do it.

DIFFICULT TO SEPARATE: If you can't easily separate the leaves of a head of lettuce or another tightly packed green vegetable, hit the stem end sharply on the counter. Then twist out the core (it should come out easily if you hit it hard enough) and run cold water vigorously into the hole you have created. The leaves will separate beautifully, not unlike a leafy green peacock.

DIRTY: For bunch greens like spinach and kale, cut the base off the bunch first—that's where most of the dirt is. Swish it around in a tub or large pot of water to loosen the dirt, eggs, bugs, and worms. Drain. Now that you've learned what might have been in your greens, you've probably thrown them in the garbage and bought some nice canned vegetables. Not to worry: washing really works. Fill your pot or tub with water again, this time with cold water, and rinse (at least three times for the really muddy stuff), draining and refreshing the rinse water until clean. If there is dirt on the bottom of your pot, your greens are still dirty.

SMELLY: If cooking greens get too smelly for your taste (or nose), add some salt to the cooking water and cook uncovered.

SPINACH IS TOO SPINACHY: Nothing else is quite as spinachy as spinach. If your spinach is too spinachy, de-spinach it by adding some curry powder, about $1/2$ teaspoon to a package of frozen spinach. If it still tastes bad, try just a little crushed pineapple. Honest.

WET: For regular loosely packed greens, let them drip into a colander; wrap them lightly in an absorbent towel, and chill. For Bibb lettuce and other full-headed greens, place them on a thick towel, cover with a kitchen towel, and chill for an hour or two.

If you need greens to be dry right away, throw them in a pillowcase and spin them dry by swinging them around in a circle outdoors, holding the pillowcase closed.

WILTED: If you've got an hour, dip the greens in hot water, then in ice water with a dash of vinegar. Shake the excess liquid from them and chill them in the refrigerator for 1 hour.

If you need them right away, unwilt them by tossing them with a few drops of oil to coat the leaves before adding the dressing.

For hopelessly wilted greens, try the following interesting recipe for hopelessly wilted greens.

Hopelessly Wilted Greens Dish

About 2 large bunches of
 hopelessly wilted greens
4 bacon slices
1/4 cup French dressing
1/4 teaspoon celery salt

2 tablespoons chopped
 chives
2 tablespoons vinegar
1 tablespoon sugar

Tear the wilted greens into bite-size pieces and put them on a plate.
Sauté the bacon and chop it into small bits. Mix the bacon with the
French dressing, celery salt, chives, vinegar, and sugar and bring to
a boil in the bacon skillet. Pour this sauce over the greens. Put the
plate of greens with sauce on top of a bowl of hot water and warm
gently for 6 minutes. Toss and serve.

GRITS

SCORCHED: As soon as you discover that the grits are burned, transfer
them to a new pot, leaving the burned part on the bottom of the old
pot. Whatever you do, don't scrape the bottom of the pot! Now, taste
the grits. If they taste scorched, they're ruined. When you start over,
remember that grits need to be stirred regularly while cooking.

TOO DRY: Add water 1 tablespoon at a time, stirring constantly until
the desired consistency is reached.

TOO WET: You probably know that if they're too wet, you should just
keep cooking until they aren't anymore.

GUACAMOLE

BROWN: Guacamole is best made just prior to eating, but if you need to
make it in advance (or you have leftovers), cover it with plastic wrap,
making sure the wrap is directly in contact with the surface of the guacamole, and chill. There might still be some slight browning when you
take it out, but it can be stirred in or scraped off. Another option is to
cover the guacamole with a layer of something that will keep the air off
of it (air being what causes the browning). We recommend something
that tastes good with guacamole, like salsa or sour cream.

HAM

CURLING: If slices of ham are starting to curl under the broiler, make a slice through the fat on the edge every inch or so. You can do this quickly and easily with scissors. It is the fat that curls, not the meat.

SALTY: Slice the ham. Soak the slices in milk for 15 to 30 minutes, then wash them off in cold water. This won't affect the taste of the ham at all, except to make it less salty.

HAMBURGERS

BLAND: Mix any of the following seasonings in with the ground meat at a rate of roughly 1 to 2 teaspoons per pound: ground allspice, celery seed, cumin, garlic powder, nutmeg, oregano, or sesame seed.

If the hamburgers are already cooked and you want to do something more inspiring than drowning them in store-bought hamburger sauce (ketchup), here are a few inspirations for covering them: bacon crumbles, guacamole, pizza sauce, shredded cheddar cheese mixed with chopped walnuts, raisin sauce, curry sauce plus chutney, sautéed onions, sour cream plus horseradish, a mound of diced stuffed green olives, or chili plus sliced black olives.

Or try one of the following truly inspirational hamburgers.

Hamburgers Bleu

Put a dollop of thick blue or Roquefort cheese dressing on the top of your cooked hamburgers. Add some crumbles of blue cheese and a strip of something red, like pimento or tomato. Broil for 3 minutes.

Hamburgers Rouge

1 small can pineapple bits	1 teaspoon soy sauce
1 heaping tablespoon ketchup	1 teaspoon cornstarch dissolved in $1/4$ cup cold water
1 tablespoon vinegar	$1/4$ cup chopped walnuts

Mix together the pineapple, ketchup, vinegar, and soy sauce. Stir in the dissolved cornstarch. Heat until thick and gooey. Pour over cooked hamburgers and toss a few nuts on top.

STUCK TO FINGERS: Dip your fingers in cold water first and raw meat won't stick to them while you're molding meatballs or sculpting replicas of the Venus de Milo, or whatever it is *you* do with ground round.

HERBS, SPICES

HAVE DRIED, NEED FRESH (OR VICE VERSA): For most herbs and spices, 1 teaspoon of fresh equals $1/3$ to $1/2$ teaspoon of dried.

NEED ONE KIND, DON'T HAVE IT: Some herbs can generally be substituted for each other as they are either similar or often found in the same kinds of dishes. However, you should expect the flavor of your dish to be affected. It's best to start with half the amount specified and then add more only after tasting. Here are some groups of herbs that may work in place of each other:

basil, oregano, thyme
cilantro, parsley
marjoram, basil, thyme, savory
parsley, tarragon, chervil
rosemary, thyme, tarragon
sage, poultry seasoning, rosemary

OLD, WEAK: Many dried herbs lose their potency after a few months; most are pretty stale within a year. One way to deal with old herbs is to rub them between your fingers for a few moments. Some spices can be renewed by cooking them in butter for a few minutes before using them. This method is especially effective with curry powder, for instance.

HOLLANDAISE SAUCE: *see* SAUCES

HONEY

CRYSTALLIZED: Heating honey will restore it to its uncrystallized state, just the way it came out of the bee. A simple way to heat it is to stand your honeypot in a pan of hot water. A faster way is to warm the honey in a microwave oven for 60 to 90 seconds per cup of honey on the high setting.

NEED SOME, HAVE NONE: In most recipes, you can substitute $1^1/_4$ cups sugar and $^1/_4$ cup of any liquid for 1 cup honey. One cup of light corn syrup can also be substituted in most baked goods.

STUCK TO CONTAINER: Next time, butter the container lightly before pouring the honey in; it won't stick at all.

HOT DOGS: *see* SAUSAGES

HUMMUS

TOO ANYTHING (GARLICKY, LEMONY, SALTY): Of course, you can add more chickpeas and process or blend until smooth. But if you happen to be out of them, another legume works nicely. White beans are particularly good. You can also add roasted red bell peppers or, if saltiness isn't the problem, black olives (either canned or kalamata).

ICE CREAM

ICY: When ice cream stored in the freezer starts to get icy or crystallized, you can often cure the problem by wrapping it very tightly in aluminum foil and returning it to the freezer for at least overnight.

MELTED: It is probably safer not to refreeze melted ice cream, and if you do, it tastes pretty dreadful anyway. What, then, do you do with it? Here are a few suggestions:

Use it on fruit as a cream sauce, if the flavors seem compatible.

Blend it with frozen fruit for an incredible milk shake–like drink. Or with fresh fruit for a darn fine smoothie.

Pour it on chunks of toasted pound cake for a Backward Sundae (the ice cream is the topping).

Or save it in the refrigerator until tomorrow morning and serve it with hot or cold cereal for a breakfast the kids will never forget.

ICE CUBES

AIR BUBBLES: Are you sure you don't have enough to worry about? All right, next time, boil the water first, pour it in the tray, let it cool to room temperature, and then put it in the freezer. No bubbles.

ICING

CRUMBY: If crumbs are coming off the cake and marring the icing, continue frosting, but apply only a very thin layer, what cake pros call a "crumb coat." Put the iced cake in the refrigerator until the icing is firm. Now, with the crumb coat holding the crumbs in place, spread a second, more beautiful, layer of icing over the cake.

GOOEY: Gooey icing is difficult to spread unless you dip the knife in very hot water before spreading and again during the spreading process, as necessary.

GRAINY: When boiled icing starts becoming grainy as it cooks, add a few drops of vinegar. This will retard the sugaring process but won't change the taste at all.

LUMPY: Icing can be lumpy because of lumps in the sugar or defects in your spreading technique. If sugar is the issue, you can press the icing through a sieve and then beat it again. That's a lot of work, though. If the problem is your spreading technique, a smooth (not serrated) knife dipped in hot water may make the process easier. Or you can cover the lumpy icing with chopped nuts or chopped or shaved chocolate, or drizzle a thin chocolate glaze over the frosted cake in a crisscross pattern, letting it run down the sides. This confuses the eye and pleases the tongue.

TOO THICK: If the icing is already made and is too thick, stir in some cream until the consistency is right.

If it gets too thick while being made, beat or stir in a few drops of lemon juice or boiling water until it becomes thinner.

TOO THIN: Add sugar (preferably confectioners' sugar), a very little at a time, stirring madly or beating it in as you do.

If, for some reason, you don't want to add sugar, beat the icing wherever there is indirect heat: in the hot sun, near an open oven door, or in the top of a double boiler.

JAM

RUNNY: If your homemade jam won't set up no matter what you do, it will still be the best syrup you ever put on your ice cream. But if you're determined to get it to gel, try this: for each cup of jam, in a saucepan, mix $1\frac{1}{2}$ teaspoons powdered pectin and 1 tablespoon water and bring to a boil, stirring. Add 2 tablespoons sugar plus your runny jam, still stirring. Bring back to a boil and boil for 1 minute. Remove from the heat and process as planned. Some fruits, such as cherries, blueberries, and apricots, are low in natural pectin. Next time you use these fruits, you may want to start out using some pectin. Or mix in a high-pectin fruit like grapes, plums, or apples. Also, less-ripe examples of your chosen fruit will have more pectin than the fully ripe stuff.

JELL-O: *see* GELATIN

JERUSALEM ARTICHOKES

MUSHY: Unfortunately, there's no way to unmush them. For now, you'll just have to make either mashed Jerusalem artichokes (just like you make mashed potatoes) or cream of Jerusalem artichoke soup (blend with some broth and cream). Next time, watch your chokes very closely, since they can turn mushy in the blink of an eye.

DISCOLORED: If the color bothers you, make them into soup or cover them with sauce. They do discolor quickly, so next time, cook or eat them immediately after cutting. If you want to prepare them in advance or eat them raw but not immediately, either toss them with an acidic dressing or soak them in acidulated water (water with lemon juice or vinegar in it). And don't cook them in an aluminum or iron pan, as both can cause discoloration.

JICAMA

WOODY: The larger ones tend to be woodier than the small ones. If the one you have is too fibrous to eat raw, try boiling and then mashing it, but frankly it won't be as tasty as one that started out tasting fresh and sweet. Use lots of butter or hot sauce.

KALE: *see* GREENS

KETCHUP: *see* SAUCES

LAMB

BLAND: Lamb is probably as compatible with a wide variety of seasonings as anything in the supermarket. Consider, among other seasonings, the following: ground allspice, caraway seeds (especially in stew), chervil, cloves (add five or six to the marinade), coriander (sparingly—$^1/_4$ teaspoon per 4 servings), cumin, dill seed, ginger, juniper berries (crush them and rub them into the lamb), mace, oregano, rosemary, or tarragon.

LAMB CHOPS CURLING: Slash the fat on the edges every half inch or so, and turn the chops over at once (you can turn them back later).

MUTTON FAT TASTES "SHEEPY": Mutton fat is great to cook with when it doesn't taste too strong. If it is too strong, add 1 part lard to 2 parts fat, chop it all up together, and melt it in a double boiler with one-fourth of its bulk in skim milk, tossing in some sweet herbs (e.g., anise, basil, marjoram, and/or mint) for good measure.

MUTTONY: When lamb tastes too strong or too muttony, try the following de-muttonizing marinade. Wipe the lamb with a damp cloth and rub with the juice of one lemon plus 2 tablespoons olive oil. Let stand for 2 hours before cooking. Use garlic when you cook it.

LARD: *see* FAT, LARD, SHORTENING

LATKES

FALLING APART: Use starchy potatoes (like russets) to make latkes, as the starch helps hold them together. If you've already used a less starchy variety, try adding extra starch in the form of matzo meal or flour. Egg may also help bind them together.

GREASY: Your oil is not hot enough. Don't crowd your latkes in the pan while cooking them, which will cause the oil temperature to drop. Soak up as much oil as you can with paper towels and serve with lots of applesauce.

SOGGY: Your oil may not have been hot enough. Or your potatoes may have been too wet. It's best to squeeze your grated potatoes in a dish towel prior to adding the other ingredients. If you've already mixed your batter, you can still try draining it in a colander. You can even still squeeze it, but then you may need to add more of some other ingredients, like your binder.

LEEKS

DIRTY: Hopefully you've noticed this as you're preparing them, not because you ended up with a mouthful of dirt at the dinner table! The layers of leeks tend to hide lots of soil. If you've halved them, soak them in water, then rinse between the layers as best you can under running water. If you've already sliced them, soak them in a bowl of water for 15 minutes, swishing them about to loosen and dislodge any grit and letting the grit settle to the bottom. Remove the leeks from the bowl with a slotted spoon and repeat as needed.

LEMONS

DRIED UP, OLD, NOT JUICY: Boil the lemon for about 5 minutes and a lot more juice—roughly one-third more—will come out. (It is better, but not vital, to let the lemon cool in the refrigerator before juicing.) Heating for 5 minutes in a 300°F oven will have the same effect, and so will 15 seconds on the high setting in a microwave oven. So, to a lesser extent, will rolling the lemon around on a tabletop with a circular pressing motion, as if you were forming balls of clay.

NEED SOME, HAVE NONE: In small quantities, 1/2 teaspoon vinegar can be substituted for 1 teaspoon lemon juice. We do not recommend this substitution when making lemonade.

PITS FALLING INTO YOUR FOOD: Wrap half a lemon in cheesecloth before squeezing. When serving dinner, do as some elegant restaurants do: knot or sew the cheesecloth shut. Very classy.

SQUIRTING: The current world's record is held by a lady from Nashville, Tennessee, who shot a stream of lemon juice 48 feet 2 inches, or across the entire width of the dance floor of the Gilded Gazebo Supper Club. Good etiquette requires you to prevent squirting by inserting a fork into your lemon wedge and squeezing it over the fork, shielding it with your hand as you do so.

LENTILS

BLAND: Lentils can be cooked in broth for a nice flavor. But let's assume they're already cooked. Lentils pair nicely with many things, including sautéed onions, garlic, tomatoes, thyme, oregano, ginger, barbecue sauce, and vinaigrette. Experiment!

MUSHY: They can't be unmushed, so your best bet may be to turn them into soup. Add broth, sautéed onions, carrots, celery, potatoes, and seasonings (see "Bland," above). You can purée some of the lentils to thicken the soup if you like. Overcooked lentils are also a great base for making veggie burgers. Consult a general or vegetarian cookbook. And just so you know, some lentils (red and yellow ones) are pretty much always mushy when cooked and tend to be best for soups and stews.

LETTUCE: *see* GREENS

LIMA BEANS: *see* BEANS, LIMA AND GREEN

LIQUEUR: *see* ALCOHOL

LIVER

BLAND: Liver, especially beef liver, isn't too compatible with many herbs and spices, although caraway seeds and juniper berries (crushed and rubbed in) do have a pleasant effect. It is better to serve the bland liver with an appropriate yummy sauce. Two sauces for beef liver and one for chicken livers are given herewith.

Creole Sauce for Beef Liver

8 ounces tomato sauce
2 tablespoons vinegar
1 tablespoon brown sugar
¼ cup chopped onion

¼ cup chopped green bell
  pepper
1 clove garlic, minced

Stir all of the ingredients together in a small saucepan, heat through, and pour it on the liver.

Mr. P.'s Beef Liver Sauce

¼ cup boiling water
¾ cup peanut butter (smooth
  or chunky)
2 teaspoons garlic salt

⅛ teaspoon cayenne pepper
Toasted sesame seeds
  (optional)

Stir the boiling water into the peanut butter to loosen it. Add the garlic salt and cayenne and stir to combine. Optionally, top the finished dish with toasted sesame seeds.

Sour Cream Sauce for Chicken Livers

FOR EACH POUND OF CHICKEN LIVERS:

1 cup sour cream
2 teaspoons lemon juice plus
  1 teaspoon chervil or
  2 teaspoons dried
  dill weed, or 1 tablespoon
  tomato purée plus
  1 teaspoon oregano

Mix all the ingredients together in a heavy saucepan and warm them slowly over low heat. Pour the sauce over the chicken livers.

POPPING, SPLATTERING: Chicken livers are wont to do this, but they won't if you prick them all over with a fork.

TOUGH: No matter what the instructions may say, meat tenderizer works as well on liver as on most other kinds of meats.

If you anticipate that your liver is going to be tough or untasty, soak it for an hour in either milk or red wine, according to your taste, and fry it in butter.

LOBSTER: *see* FISH AND SEAFOOD

LOGANBERRIES: *see* BERRIES

MACARONI: *see* PASTA

MANGOES

DIFFICULT TO PEEL: All mangoes are difficult to peel from one end and easy to peel from the other end. As the famous calypso song goes, "If your mango hard to peel/I got for you, mon, such a deal/If this side doesn't work my friend/Simply try the other end." If you have a really reluctant mango, try a vegetable peeler. Last resort: use a serrated knife, sawing back and forth very carefully. Hold the mango in a dish towel (so it doesn't slip) over a sink (in case it drips).

UNRIPE: Put unripe mangoes in a paper bag and keep them in a warm place until they ripen.

MAPLE SYRUP

NEED SOME, HAVE NONE: For baking, you can substitute sugar: 1 cup sugar plus 2 tablespoons liquid appropriate for the dish would equal the sweetness and moisture of ³/₄ cup maple syrup. Of course, it will not have the same flavor, so if you have maple flavoring on hand, add some. If you need maple syrup for pancakes, you can try the following syrup recipe. It won't taste as good as real maple syrup (keep in mind that fruit, fruit sauce, chocolate sauce, peanut butter and honey, and jam are all great spooned, spread, or poured over pancakes), but it *will* coat your pancakes in sticky sweetness.

Pancake Syrup

1/2 cup granulated sugar	3/4 cup corn syrup
1/2 cup brown sugar	1/2 teaspoon maple flavoring
1/2 cup water	or vanilla extract

In a saucepan, combine the sugars, water, and corn syrup and bring to a boil over medium-high heat. Boil for 2 minutes and stir in the maple flavoring before serving.

MARSHMALLOWS

HARD, STALE: Seal them up in an airtight container (like a plastic bag) with a slice of fresh bread for 3 days and you will have fresh marshmallows and stale bread.

STUCK TO UTENSIL WHILE CUTTING: Dip the scissors (you were using scissors, weren't you?) in cold water and cut the marshmallows while the blades are still wet.

MAYONNAISE

NOT ENOUGH: In things like egg salad or on sandwiches, stir in some ketchup or chile sauce, if the taste is compatible. If not, thin out the mayonnaise (see "Too Thick," below) and increase the seasoning in the salad. Or make your own mayonnaise (as long as salmonella is not a concern). It's unbelievably easy using a blender or food processor. Here's how.

Mayonnaise

1 egg, at room temperature
1/2 teaspoon powdered
mustard
1/4 teaspoon salt
2 tablespoons vinegar

1 cup canola oil (or experiment with oils such as olive
and peanut for a different
flavor)

Add the egg, mustard, salt, vinegar, and 1/4 cup of the canola oil to a blender or food processor and process until well combined. With the motor running, add the remaining oil in a slow, steady stream until all the oil has been added and the mixture is thick and creamy.

SEPARATED: Rinse a bowl using hot water and dry it. Add 1 teaspoon prepared mustard, 1 egg yolk, and 1 teaspoon of the separated mayonnaise and beat with a whisk until creamy. Add another teaspoon of the mayonnaise and repeat. Continue adding the separated mayonnaise, 1 teaspoon at a time, until you have a nice thick, unseparated mayonnaise.

TOO THICK: Thin it out with cream, whipped cream, evaporated milk, or lemon juice, whichever is handy. Used in small amounts, none of these will flavor the mayonnaise. If you would like to flavor it, you can thin it out with fruit juice. The juice from a cantaloupe or watermelon is especially interesting. To lower the fat content, consider substituting nonfat sour cream or yogurt for some of the mayonnaise in a dressing.

MEAT: *see specific meat*

MEAT LOAF

BLAND: All of these seasonings (used one or two at a time, please) go nicely with meat loaf: ground allspice, celery seed, coriander, fennel, garlic powder, nutmeg, oregano, paprika, and sesame seeds. Also see the next suggestion.

STUCK TO THE PAN: This time, scrape it out as best you can with a spatula and reassemble it, using sauce to hold it together.

Next time, put a strip or two of partly cooked bacon underneath the meat loaf before cooking. Not only will it not stick, but it also won't taste like bacon. If you want your meat loaf to be bacon-flavored, drape the rest of the package of bacon over the top. This works for de-blanding, too.

MELONS

BLAND: Some melons, such as cantaloupe and honeydew, benefit from a light salting. Really. Some lime juice and chile powder isn't bad either. Can't bring yourself to? How about a squeeze of lemon or orange juice? You can also try turning a bland melon into a sorbet or granita. Make sure you use intense flavorings to help mask your melon's shortcomings.

MERINGUE

DIFFICULT TO CUT: Dip the knife in very cold water.

DISINTEGRATING, CRACKED: Best to make a pavlova, the New Zealand national dessert. Assemble the bits in a ring mold, using a liberal amount of whipped cream to stick the pieces together. Once you turn the meringue mixture out of the mold, fill the center of the ring with whipped cream. Top with fresh fruit, such as kiwi, berries, or well-drained mandarin orange slices.

WEEPING: We hate to see a grown meringue cry. It tends to do so when it is cooled too fast. Cool it very slowly by leaving it in the oven as the oven cools, for instance, and it will weep no more.

MILK: *see also* CREAM

NEED SOME, HAVE NONE: If you don't have evaporated milk on your emergency shelf, then for most uses (including drinking, but especially cooking) you can substitute the following for 1 cup of whole milk: 1 cup buttermilk plus $1/2$ teaspoon baking soda, or 1 cup skim milk plus 2 teaspoons oil or fat. If you need sour milk, add 1 teaspoon lemon juice or cider vinegar to 1 cup regular milk.

In baking, depending on the recipe, fruit juice can sometimes be substituted for milk. Apple juice is the most neutral-tasting.

SOURING: Add 2 teaspoons baking soda to a quart of milk and it will be good for another day or two.

MILLET

BLAND: Millet's flavor can be improved by toasting it prior to cooking and by cooking it in broth instead of water. Cooked millet can be mixed with various flavorings, like butter, garlic, chile peppers or oil, scallions, caramelized onions, a hard grating cheese (like Parmesan), or perhaps all of the above.

MISO

BLAND: Miso tends to lose its flavor with age. How long has that container been lurking in the back of your fridge? For now, as long as you're not making miso soup (if you are, then stop reading this and go to the store to buy some fresh miso), use the bland miso that you have, but try boosting its flavor with some soy sauce, black bean sauce, or sesame oil or paste.

MOLASSES

NEED SOME, HAVE NONE: In baking, for 1 cup of molasses, you can substitute an equal amount of honey or dark corn syrup, or $3/4$ cup dark brown sugar plus $1/4$ cup water. The flavor of your recipe will, of course, change somewhat.

STUCK TO CONTAINER: Next time, butter the container lightly before putting the molasses in it and the molasses will roll right off. Now, put the container in a larger container with hot water in it. Warmed molasses is thinner and will unstick.

MOUSSE

DOESN'T SET: It isn't mousse anymore; now it's a sauce to serve over an appropriate fruit or cubed cake. It's also probably a great sauce.

MUFFINS: *see also* BREAD AND ROLLS

SOGGY BOTTOMS: This happens because moisture in the muffins condenses in the bottom of the muffin pan after cooking. Counteract this by putting the muffins on a rack to cool or by simply turning them sideways in their little compartments when you take them out of the oven to cool.

STUCK TO THE MUFFIN PAN: Put the muffin pan on a wet towel. In a couple of minutes, the muffins should come free.

TOUGH: Tough muffins (which are not the same as tough cookies) probably got that way because you beat the batter rather than folded it. This time, cut your muffins into slices, toast, and serve with jam. Next time, fold the batter, or stir very briefly, just until the wet and dry ingredients are combined.

MUSHROOMS

BLAND: The best seasoning to bring out the flavor in mushrooms is marjoram. Add a generous dash to cooking mushrooms. No marjoram? Excuse me, have you got the thyme?

DARKENING, TOO DARK: If your mushrooms are dark and you don't want them to mar a light-colored sauce, wipe them with a damp cloth, rub them with lemon juice, and store them in the refrigerator. Or steam them in milk or butter in the top of a double boiler for 20 minutes. Or, while cooking, add a few drops of lemon juice to the cooking liquid. (It is just about impossible to lighten mushrooms in a black iron skillet.)

SHRIVELED: Peel them with your fingers. Beneath every shriveled mushroom there lies a somewhat smaller smooth mushroom waiting to be found. (Use the peelings to flavor soups or sauces.)

TOO LIGHT: Mushrooms will darken if cooked in butter in a black iron skillet over high heat.

TOO MANY: Chop them and then cook very slowly over low heat until they are reduced by half or more. Now you have duxelle, a mushroom paste that stores well in the refrigerator. Use it where mushroom flavoring is required, for example, in sauces, soups, and stews.

MUSHROOM SOUP: *see* SOUPS

MUSSELS: *see also* CLAMS; OYSTERS

UNCERTAIN QUALITY: Steam mussels for 10 minutes. If they open up, they're good. If they don't, they're bad.

MUSTARD

NEED SOME, HAVE NONE: Do you have any powdered mustard? You can make your own prepared mustard by mixing 1^{1}/$_{2}$ tablespoons powdered mustard with ^{1}/$_{2}$ cup water, ^{1}/$_{4}$ cup vinegar, and ^{1}/$_{4}$ cup white wine. The longer you let it sit, the mellower it will taste. At least a couple hours is recommended. (Of course, in that time you could run to the store for a jar of mustard.)

MUSTARD GREENS: *see* GREENS

NECTARINES

UNRIPE: To accelerate ripening, store them sealed in a brown paper bag for 1 or 2 days. Set them where the sun can warm the bag.

NOODLES: *see* PASTA

NORI

STALE: You can try to recrisp stale sheets of nori by waving them across a lit gas burner, one at a time (careful, please). We admit to having made sushi with stale nori and nobody seemed to notice (or were too polite to mention it). It will be slightly tougher than if it were fresh, but it should still be usable. Next time, store it in an airtight bag in the freezer to keep it fresh longer.

NUTS

CRUMBLY: If nut meats crumble when you crack the shells, soak the remaining unshelled nuts in salt water overnight.

DIFFICULT TO CRACK, SHELL: For pecans and similar nuts, cover them with boiling water and let stand until cold. Crack the nuts end-to-end with a nutcracker and the meat should emerge in one piece.

For chestnuts, make a small gash on the flat side of the nut, penetrating the outer skin. Roast in a 400°F oven until the skins loosen, or cover with cold water and bring to a boil. Remove and let stand until cool enough to handle. The shells and skins should be easier to remove.

DIFFICULT TO PEEL, SKIN, REMOVE NUT MEAT: For almonds and similar nuts, drop the whole nut (shelled) into boiling water and let stand for 3 minutes with the heat off. The skins (that is, the brown layer on the nut meat) should come off easily. Dry the nut meats on a towel.

NEED SOME, HAVE NONE: In brownies and similar items, coarse bran can successfully be substituted for nuts.

To substitute for nuts in molasses cake, spice cake, and stuff of that ilk, brown a cup of rolled oats by spreading them on a baking sheet in a 425°F oven, watching carefully to be sure that they don't burn. Add the oats before baking the cake.

In many baked goods, other bits, like chocolate chips, peanut butter chips, or raisins (or other dried fruits), are a fine substitute.

RANCID: There's not much to do with rancid nuts except compost them. Next time, store your nuts in an airtight bag or container in the refrigerator or freezer to keep them fresher longer.

SHELLS MIXED IN WITH NUTS: Dump the whole works in a bowl of water. The shells will float, the meat will sink, and the guppies will swim around in the middle.

NUT FLOURS AND MEALS

HAVE ONE, NEED THE OTHER: Nut meals are just ground nuts. Nut flours are also ground nuts, but the oil has been pressed out. They can be substituted for each other in baked goods, but meals will result in a coarser texture.

If you grind your own meal, keep an eye on it. If you grind it for too long, you will end up with a nut butter—which is a fine thing to eat, but not what you were going for.

OATS: *see also* CEREALS

NEED SOME, HAVE NONE: In baking, 1 cup all-purpose flour can replace 1^1/$_3$ cups oats. If you have any cereal flakes, consider substituting those. Cornflake-raisin cookies are not bad at all, as long as you don't apologize while serving them.

If you have old-fashioned oats but need quick-cooking oats, process them briefly in a food processor or blender, just until they're coarsely chopped.

OCTOPUS

TOUGH: Octopus should be tenderized before cooking. Generally, cookbooks suggest you do this simply by precooking it. Simmer it until it's tender (about 1 hour, though a very large octopus could take up to twice as long; conversely, a very small one may take less time), and then continue with your recipe. If you haven't done this, you can just keep cooking it however you've started, keeping in mind that sometimes it takes hours for octopus to become tender. Test it regularly, though, because if it's cooked for too long, it will become dry and tasteless. If you've ended up with octopus chewing gum, your only options are to dump it in the compost or serve it without apology.

If you don't have time for a long cook right now, you might want to store it in the freezer until you're ready to use it. Some say freezing octopus helps tenderize it.

OIL

RANCID: There's really nothing you can do with rancid oil except replace it. Oxygen, heat, and light can all play a factor in turning an oil rancid. Your best bet is to store your oils in airtight containers in a cool, dark place. Some experts believe that all oils should be kept in the refrigerator, but others argue that doing so can affect the appearance and flavor. Even properly cared for, oil does have an expiration date, so keep track of yours.

SMOKING: When oil starts smoking it means that it has overheated and started breaking down. It could be producing substances that you don't want to put in your healthy body, so toss it out and start over. Different oils have different smoke points. For high-heat cooking, use an oil with a high smoke point. Canola and safflower are among the highest.

OKRA

GUMMY OR SLIMY: We assume you're cooking sliced okra. The pod makes a sort of gummy liquid when cut and cooked. This can be done intentionally to thicken a stew (think gumbo). If it doesn't work for you, cook the pods, preferably small ones, whole next time. Or fry the slices, dredged in cornmeal. This time, if you're making plain okra, perhaps you'd enjoy them more mixed with another vegetable. Tomatoes go well with okra, as do onions and peppers.

OLIVES

HARD TO PIT: Place them on a paper towel or wax paper. Roll gently with a rolling pin. Press the olive with the heel of your hand and the pit will pop out.

OMELETTES: *see also* EGGS *(various subcategories)*

STUCK TO PAN: Remove the eggs as best you can, preferably with a wooden implement (no, not your cane), and either 1) cover the bits with an appropriate sauce, or 2) save them as a garnish to use on dishes such as fried rice.

Next time, grease the pan with unsalted butter or oil. Salted butter is more likely to cause things to stick.

ONIONS

BLAND: Dried basil, sage, and thyme and ground ginger are all good seasonings to add to bland cooking onions—or just butter and lightly sugar them.

CRYING WHILE PEELING OR SLICING: For many, the best solution is to chill the onions. If you have time, put the onions in the freezer for 10 to 15 minutes before slicing. Alternatively, you can peel them under water (just the onion and your hands, no scuba gear needed) or under cold running water. For some people, biting on a piece of bread seems to help, for others not at all. Those of us desperately sensitive to chopping onions have been known to use our snorkeling mask when chopping many onions, or even to use the food processor for just one onion (the cleanup is worth it). Cutting next to an open flame, whether from a candle or your gas stove, can also be helpful. Finally, make sure your knife is nice and sharp. This will cut down on the enzymes being released from your onions, which become the gas that hurts your eyes.

DIFFICULT TO PEEL: Hot water loosens onion peels. Drop onions in boiling water for somewhere between 10 seconds (for tiny white onions) and 5 minutes (for big old red ones) and then dip them in cold water; the peel will virtually fall off.

FALLING APART WHILE COOKING: We mean the onions, and not you, of course. When cooking whole pearl onions or *cipollini*, cut an X on the root end of the onion with a sharp knife and it will help hold loose onions together. (The root end is usually flatter, and it has a little dark spot where the root was.)

SAUTÉING UNEVENLY: You have a recipe that calls for browned onions, but as you brown them, some are dark brown while others are still white. Sprinkle the onions with a bit of sugar as they cook and they should sauté evenly thereafter.

SMELLY: Spicy smells tend to overcome oniony smells. The simplest spicy smell maker is a few cloves simmering in a pan of vinegar.

TOO SOFT: Boiled onions that have become too soft can be firmed up again by dipping them briefly in ice water.

TOO STRONG: If you're using them raw, rinse the onions under cold water to make them less strong. If you're cooking them, increase the cooking time over low heat. The longer they cook, the mellower they will be.

WILTING: When green onions start wilting, you can revive them by replanting them! Simply stick the root end in the ground and it will take root and grow healthy again. This does not work, alas, with most other things, including human beings.

ORANGES

BLAND: Vanilla is delightfully compatible with orange flavor, as the Dreamsicle people learned years ago. Add a tiny bit of vanilla extract to your indifferently flavored oranges, and to indifferently flavored orange juice as well.

DIFFICULT TO PEEL: Pour boiling water over the oranges and let them stand for 5 minutes. The peels will come off very easily, and so will all the white pith under the peel. The peel is permanently loosened by this technique, so you can do it in advance and still refrigerate the oranges. This process also tends to make the oranges considerably juicier.

NOT JUICY: See "Difficult to Peel," above. Or roll the oranges around on a table, as if you were trying to make them rounder. That really loosens up the old juices.

OYSTERS: *see also* CLAMS

CAN'T SHUCK: The colder the oyster, the easier it is to shuck. Keep your oysters in the refrigerator until you're ready to shuck them. Use a good sturdy oyster knife and a twisting motion while opening.

SANDY: Sprinkle them with lots of cornmeal and then cover with cold water. Let stand for about 3 hours, then rinse well.

PANCAKES

COLD AND SOGGY: Pancakes can be reheated by placing them between the folds of a clean dish towel in a 250°F oven.

LEFTOVER: Leftover pancakes freeze well. Let them cool completely first or they will stick to whatever you're freezing them in. You can then either stack them, separated by pieces of waxed paper, and store them in a freezer bag, or you can freeze them flat on a baking sheet and then stack them without the waxed paper. When you want to serve them, brush the frozen pancakes with melted butter and reheat in a 350°F oven or toaster oven. Or pop in the toaster, in which case we don't recommend buttering first. (The toaster method is more convenient, but it will make the outsides a little tougher.) The Scots, however, consider leftover pancakes to be just a kind of soft crumpet to be served with butter and jam for tea. You might do the same. Or you could make sandwiches—how about with cream cheese softened with fruit juice? Peanut butter and jelly is nice. Peanut butter and banana is even better. One cookbook suggests cutting them into strips and using them as you would use noodles. Hmm. Or perhaps you could sail them around the backyard as Frisbees.

STUCK TO THE GRIDDLE: Usually this means they aren't fatty enough. Next batch, add a little more butter or shortening.

PANS: *see* Appendix F.

PAPAYAS

BLAND: Sprinkle with a splash of citrus juice, a bit of sugar, and a touch of rum!

OVERRIPE: You can keep a papaya in the refrigerator to slow its ripening, but if it's already too soft, purée it and use it in ice cream, in a custard, in a marinade (papaya contains a meat-tenderizing enzyme), or on your morning yogurt. (Don't forget that the seeds are edible, too. Blend them into a salad dressing.)

UNRIPE: Close up papayas in a brown paper bag to help them ripen more quickly.

PARSLEY

DIFFICULT TO CHOP: Wash it very briefly in hot water and dry it off with paper towels. Its chopability quotient should rise noticeably. Also, don't forget that very handy kitchen implement called the scissors.

PARSNIPS

BITTER OR WOODY: This is a problem common to large and old parsnips. The core is the woodiest and most bitter part, so cut the parsnip lengthwise into wedges and trim away and discard the cores.

MUSHY: They're overcooked. Turn them into mashed parsnips, in the same way you'd make mashed potatoes.

NOT ENOUGH: Substitute carrots.

PASTA

BOILING OVER: The immediate remedy is to blow on the surface of the water. This will give you about a 15 seconds' grace period to look frantically around for the pot holder to pull the pot off the burner. If you can't find it, blow again. And again. Then put a bit of oil (about 1 tablespoon) in the water. Next time, lightly grease the top inch of the inside of the pot.

MUSHY: Sauté the mushy drained pasta in a skillet in some olive oil until a bit browned. It will give it a bit more bite.

STUCK TOGETHER: If your drained pasta is stuck together, you can unstick it by quickly plunging it back into boiling water, this time with a healthy glug of olive oil or some butter in the water. Next time, put the oil in at the start and the problem won't arise. Also, make sure you cook the pasta in plenty of rapidly boiling water and stir it occasionally.

If the pasta is permanently stuck together—this can happen with lasagna noodles, for instance—slice the mass thin to make new noodles and use them as you had planned. You can also fry the new noodles with a butter-and-oil mixture and some onions, using the same sauce you had originally planned.

PASTRY: *see also* PUFF PASTRY

EDGES BROWNING TOO FAST: Cover just the edges with a thin strip of aluminum foil, shaped to fit.

TOO CRUMBLY TO ROLL: Lightly gather it together on the pastry board, cover it with a slightly dampened cloth, and let it rest for 10 minutes. Now try again. If it's still too crumbly, throw caution to the wind and add more liquid—only a bit at a time, though—until it's rollable.

TOO MUCH: Unbaked pastry can be frozen, thus providing a head start on your next pie or casserole. Baked pastry, such as empty pie shells, freeze well, too. Both an oven and a microwave are perfect for reheating.

TOUGH: You can't untoughen a baked pie crust. If it's inedibly tough, just scoop out the insides of whatever you've made (perform this procedure in the kitchen, not at the table) and serve them with ice cream or whipped cream. Overworking makes pastry tough, so use a light hand when mixing. If you think your unbaked pastry dough may be overworked (your 5-year-old insisted on helping!), rolling it out as thin as possible will make its toughness less obvious.

PEA SOUP: *see* SOUPS

PEACHES

DARKENING: Sprinkle them with lemon juice after peeling to retard the approaching darkness.

DIFFICULT TO PEEL: Firm peaches can be peeled just like potatoes using a potato peeler, which may then be called a peach peeler. Soft peaches can be peeled like tomatoes by dunking them for about 3 minutes in water that you've brought to a boil and then removed from the stove. The peel should then come off quite easily.

Or you can microwave a peach on the high setting for 10 seconds and let it stand for 5 minutes before peeling.

FUZZY: Say, do you remember those television commercials where they used to shave a peach? (They were selling electric razors, not bald peaches.) If your peach is very ripe and very fuzzy, that may be your only solution. (Does anyone know how to get peach fuzz out of an electric razor?) For less ripe peaches, scrub them with a vegetable brush and they will ripen into clean-shaven peaches.

NEED PEACHES, HAVE NECTARINES: In a recipe, you can substitute nectarines for peaches, but add a bit of juice (whatever you have handy—orange, apple, or pineapple), as nectarines tend to be less juicy than peaches.

UNRIPE: Store them in a closed paper bag for 1 or 2 days.

PEANUT BUTTER

SEPARATING: Turn the jar upside down and put it back on the shelf.

TOO THICK: If the jar is glass, heating it (without the lid, please) in the microwave for 30 seconds or so will soften most peanut butters. Or peanut butter can be thinned with one of these five peanut butter thinners: soft butter, cooking oil, maple syrup, hot water, or orange juice. Or, if the sandwich isn't going to be eaten until later or if you happen to like frozen peanut butter sandwiches, you can freeze the bread first so that it doesn't tear when it's spread with stiff peanut butter.

PEARS

RIPENING TOO FAST: Refrigerate them. The colder they are, the slower they will ripen.

RIPENING TOO SLOWLY: Store them in a closed brown paper bag for 1 or 2 days.

TOO MANY: Make pear sauce. It's much like apple sauce. Only pear-y.

PEAS

BLAND: All five of the following seasonings are said to pep up tired old peas: basil, marjoram, poppy seeds, rosemary, and sage. Or combine peas with minced onions that have been browned in butter. (You may call this dish peas *lyonnaise*.)

FROZEN TO THE BOX: Run cold tap water into the spaces in the box and the peas should come rolling out.

THAWED: See Appendix B to help you decide what to do about peas that have thawed out too soon.

UNCERTAIN QUALITY: Drop dried peas in water. The bad ones will float and the good ones will sink to the bottom.

PECANS: *see* NUTS

PEPPER: *see* SALT, PEPPER

PEPPERS, GREEN: *see* BELL PEPPERS

PERSIMMONS

TOO MANY: Make this delightfully simple dessert.

Persimmon Sorbet

Peel the persimmons and remove the seeds (unless you have the seedless kind, in which case you're off the hook). Freeze the persimmon meat. When it is frozen, put it in a food processor and process until it is mushy. Eat.

UNRIPE: Here is an astonishing method for overnight ripening of unripe persimmons. The only reason it didn't make page-one headlines is that so few newspaper editors like persimmons. Wrap the unripe persimmon in aluminum foil. Put it in the freezer. When it is frozen solid, remove it and allow it to thaw at room temperature. When it is thawed out, it will be ripe. Stop the presses!

PESTO

DISCOLORED: Contact with the air will turn your pesto an unattractive brown. Scoop off this top layer and store the pesto either covered in a thin layer of olive oil or with plastic wrap pressed directly onto the surface.

PHYLLO

DRY: Phyllo is finicky stuff. The sheets are paper thin, and they dry out and turn brittle very quickly. The faster you work, the better. Cover the phyllo you're not using with either plastic wrap or a damp towel and remove only as many sheets as you'll be working with right away.

STUCK TOGETHER: If you've made your own phyllo, we're very impressed and we can't help you because you're out of our league. Most of us buy it frozen and thaw it. If the sheets are stuck together, they may not be fully thawed. Continue to thaw. And always thaw phyllo in the refrigerator, or condensation may be your issue (in which case you may need to see "Torn," below).

TORN: Depending on what you're making, you may be able to use torn pieces. As long as they don't form the top layer, no one will be able to tell once the dish is cooked. Just fit the pieces together as best you can. If your phyllo is hopelessly in pieces, never fear: you can still make something delicious with it. You can crumble it up and mix it with butter or margarine. Use it to top a casserole. Or add sugar and top a pie or tart.

Or make these phyllo nests.

Phyllo Nests

Generally, recipes for phyllo nests call for *kataifi*, a kind of phyllo sold already shredded into beautifully fine strips. But using torn phyllo is more fun (if not quite as pretty).

Cut your scraps into some semblance of strips. Gently toss your strips with melted butter. For each nest you will need about 1/2 cup phyllo strips and 2 teaspoons melted butter (don't worry about being super-exact). Fit this mix into greased muffin cups, molding it up the sides as best you can. Bake in a 350°F oven for 10 to 15 minutes, or until golden brown. Let cool. Fill with fruit. Or pudding.

PICKLES

NOT PICKLED ENOUGH: Put them back in the jar with a bunch of dill, unless there is already dill in the jar. The longer they sit, the more pickled they will get, until eventually they may burn a hole right though the jar.

SCUM IN THE JAR: Float 1 teaspoon olive oil on the surface of the liquid in the jar and the scum will go away, never to return.

PIES: *see also* CAKES; COOKIES; CREAM PUFFS; PASTRY

BLAND: Ground allspice is a fine pepper-upper for most kinds of pies, including apple, berry, raisin, pumpkin, prune, and custard, among others. Add 1/4 teaspoon to the filling to start with.

Caraway seeds in the crust give apple pie a different and interesting taste. Add 1 teaspoon per 2 cups of flour. Two other good things to add: cumin to the fruit of a fruit pie before putting on the top crust; fennel sprinkled on top of the crust before baking.

DRYING OUT WHILE COOKING: Erecting a small smokestack in the center of the pie permits the heat to escape, so it doesn't stay inside and boil the juices away. The simplest sort of smokestack is a piece of raw macaroni inserted vertically, right in the middle of the pie.

If the pie has already dried out too much, you can fix it with a simple syrup (see the following recipes), adding a dash of rum or cognac if it suits your fancy, pouring it through the slashes in the crust.

Simple Syrup

1/2 cup sugar
1 cup water

Combine the sugar and the water in a saucepan. Cover and bring to a boil. Uncover and simmer for 3 minutes. Store leftover syrup in the refrigerator.

Simpler Syrup

1/4 cup currant jelly
1/2 cup water

Stir them together and heat until boiling.

Simplest Syrup

Maple syrup

Use it straight from the bottle.

FILLING TOO LOOSE (FRUIT PIES): This is a common problem. The immediate fix is to serve the runny pie à la mode, spooning the juices like a sauce over the ice cream and acting like that was part of the plan all along.

Next time, use a different recipe. Or do as some bakers do and toss the fruit with a bit of sugar, let the fruit sit until it gives up some juice, then pour off the juice before filling the pie (the juice is yummy so don't throw it away—pour it over your pancakes or something). Other bakers cook the fruit on the stove top until it's thickened prior to pouring it into the crust. And others use multiple thickeners (cornstarch *and* tapioca or cornstarch *and* flour). One trick that's great for berry pies is to add a grated apple to the filling. You won't see or taste the apple in the baked pie, but the pectin in the apple will help the filling gel. This may work with other fruit pies (hopefully you don't need a trick for your apple pie), but we've not tried it. Always let your pie cool completely before serving. Yes, it may taste great warm, but the filling will have the best texture once it has cooled.

HOT: The traditional way of cooling pies is to put them on the windowsill, from which they will be stolen by cute freckle-faced boys. Now that the windowsill is going the way of the running board, pies may be cooled quickly by putting a layer of ice cubes in a big pan and resting the pie tin on top of the ice cubes.

NOT ENOUGH FILLING: Shorten the side crust to the top of the filling and serve it as a flan or as a tart with a lattice crust.

SOGGY CRUST: Consider serving the pie by scooping out the filling, leaving the soggy crust behind. If it was a cream pie, it's now pudding; if it was a fruit pie, it's now fruit compote for ice cream! Next time, before adding the filling, brush the bottom and sides of the pastry with a beaten (but not fluffy) egg white, and put it in a 400°F oven for about 4 minutes. Or bake your pie on the bottom of the oven or on a pizza stone.

TOO SWEET: Add the juice of half a lemon to the filling. This also helps to bring out the flavor of the fruit, especially in berry pies.

PINEAPPLES

DIFFICULT TO PEEL: It can be difficult if you don't have one of those $3 billion machines they use in pineapple factories. So how about slicing the pineapple first and then cutting away the peel and the core afterward? Much easier.

UNRIPE: Pineapples do not ripen further after harvesting. However, they may start breaking down, which will make them softer and juicier (hey, it's *something* if you've got an unripe one). Speed up the process by sealing the pineapple in a brown paper bag and storing it in a warm (not hot) place. Some say you can tell a ripe pineapple when one of the center leaves pulls out easily, but this isn't always true. It depends on how the pineapple has been stored. A ripe pineapple will smell mildly of pineapple at the bottom. Too strong a smell indicates that it's overripe.

PINE NUTS: *see* NUTS

PITA

NO POCKET: Pita bread is also called pocket bread, so it should have a pocket. But your homemade pita is pocketless? Pita needs to cook at a fairly high temperature to create the steam that causes the pita to puff, so make sure that your oven is hot enough (450°F works well). Also, don't peek during baking, because if you open the door to the oven too soon, not only will the oven temperature drop, you'll release the steam. (But the rounds do cook quickly, so don't wait too long.) We know these tricks, but 8.6 percent of the pita we make still comes out without a pocket. Why? Who knows? They are still delicious cut into wedges and piled with whatever we were originally planning to stuff into them.

PIZZA

BURNED: It is almost always the crust and not the topping that gets burned. Scrape off the topping onto another pizza, or toast if you're in a hurry, or stir into a macaroni casserole.

TOO GUNKY TO CUT: Sometimes pizzas are so gunky that even those circular pizza cutters won't work effectively. In such cases, try cutting the pizza apart with ordinary kitchen scissors. (You can even use out-of-the-ordinary kitchen scissors, if that's what you have.) Or you can just wait. If it sits for a while, your pizza will firm up. But who are we kidding? Who can wait for pizza?

POI

NOT SOUR ENOUGH OR TOO SOUR: Poi (cooked mashed taro root) can be eaten fresh (not sour) or fermented (sour). If you've just mashed homemade poi and want it sour, let it age for 2 or 3 days at room temperature or in the refrigerator until it's as sour as you like. If you've gotten carried away and now it's too sour, you can add a little sugar to taste, as long as you don't admit it to any actual Hawaiians. Refrigeration will slow the souring process, freezing even more.

POLENTA

BLAND: Polenta tends to be fairly bland when cooked by itself in water. If you've already cooked it and find it too bland, your best bet is to top it with something interesting. see "Too Much," below, for a few suggestions. If you want to try cooking it with a bit more oomph, you can sauté some garlic or onion in the pot before adding the polenta and liquid. You can also cook the polenta in broth instead of water. Thyme, basil, and oregano are all herbs that marry nicely with polenta. And, believe it or not, poppy seeds are also a fine addition.

LUMPY: Whisk it vigorously as it cooks. If it seems hopeless, try whirring it in a food processor.

TOO MUCH: Spread it in a greased baking dish, refrigerate it until firm, then slice it and fry in oil. Top with marinara sauce and some provolone or perhaps some sautéed peppers. Adding some olives, mushrooms, and/or zucchini would not be a bad thing; serving it with ratatouille would be nice as well. Sautéed greens drizzled with balsamic vinegar are also quite pleasant on top of polenta.

TOO THIN OR TOO THICK: Polenta can be cooked with a water-to-polenta ratio of 6:1 for very soft, to 3:1 for very firm. If it's too loose, just keep cooking until the moisture evaporates and it's the texture you want. If it's too thick, add warm liquid while continuously stirring. The polenta will firm up as it cools.

POMEGRANATES

HARD TO SEED: Cut the pomegranate into quarters. Place sections in a bowl of water and gently roll out the seeds with your fingers, bending the skin back as necessary. The seeds will sink and the membranes will float.

HAVE POMEGRANATE, NEED POMEGRANATE JUICE: You can cut and juice a pomegranate using a handheld juicer, much as you would a citrus fruit. Or you can blend the seeds in a blender and then strain out the solids.

POPCORN

WON'T POP: The usual reason regular (not microwave) popcorn won't pop is that it is too dry. Soak the kernels in water for 5 minutes, drain them, and try again.

If this doesn't work, an almost certain remedy is to freeze the kernels for 24 hours or more and pop them while they are still frozen. (Some people store their popcorn in the freezer for just this reason.)

POPOVERS

COLLAPSED: Serve them anyway. They will still taste delicious. Next time, make sure all your batter ingredients are at room temperature, don't overfill the cups with batter, and for goodness' sake, don't open the oven door while they're baking!

LEFTOVER: Cut them in half and fill with whipped cream and berries. Or ice cream and chocolate sauce.

SOGGY: Turn them upside down in their cups and put them back in the oven for 5 minutes. Next time, prick them with a fork or knife as soon as they come out of the oven so that the steam that caused them to puff up is released before it can turn the popovers soggy.

PORK

BLAND: These seasonings go best with pork: caraway seeds, cardamom (about 1 teaspoon per 4 servings), chervil, cloves (four or five in the marinade), coriander, cumin, fennel (rub $1/2$ teaspoon onto a roast), juniper berries, marjoram, oregano, paprika, rosemary, and sage.

DRY: Slice it and place in a pan. Bring some some stock, broth, bouillon, or whatever to a boil and pour it over the meat. Cover and let sit for a few minutes. Hopefully it will soak up some of the moisture.

SALTY: If salt pork is too salty, blanch it by dropping it into water that is just simmering for 2 minutes. When you remove it, plunge it into a bowl of cold water to stop it from cooking. You can do this with a big chunk of salt pork or with small pieces. Lower small pieces into the water in a sieve so they'll be easier to retrieve.

POT ROAST

FATTY: If your pot roast really looks too fatty to be acceptable, cook it well, chill it in the refrigerator, remove the now-solidified fat, and return it to the pot, or wherever it was.

TOUGH: In addition to the usual meat tenderizers, you might consider adding tomatoes to the pot the roast is cooking in. The acid in tomatoes breaks down the fibers in the meat, thereby tenderizing it. If you don't have 3 hours to simmer the roast, slice it very thin, put it back in the pot for 15 minutes, and then serve.

POTATOES

BAKED, COLD: Baked potatoes can be reheated without overcooking by dipping them in cold water, then putting them into a 350°F oven for 10 to 15 minutes.

BAKED, EXPLODING: This time, duck! If you're not concerned about their appearance, serve the exploded potatoes. If you are concerned, turn them into mashed potatoes. Next time, cut a slice in the potato, or puncture it to let the steam escape, thereby preventing explosions.

BAKED, FAST METHOD: Parboiling for 5 minutes before baking, or sticking one of those potato nails (or any big aluminum nail) through the potato will cut the baking time by about 20 minutes. Of course, some people consider the 5-minute baked potato sufficient reason for owning a microwave oven. But keep in mind that using a microwave won't yield the nice thick browned skin that some of us consider the reason to eat a baked potato.

BOILED, BLAND: Add a pinch of rosemary or a bay leaf to the cooking liquid. Or top the potatoes with sour cream to which you have added a pinch of marjoram.

BOILED, DISINTEGRATING: If you were boiling the potatoes for a picnic potato salad, add extra crunchy bits like celery, chopped green onions, and dill pickle. Combine everything and add it to the potatoes. Toss lightly and then spoon into a bowl or mold and tamp it down. Chill. Turn it out and decorate with parsley. A triumph from a disaster.

BOILED, OLD AND STALE: Add a slice of lemon to the cooking water. It tends to prevent discoloring and helps bring out what flavor remains.

BOILED, SKIN STICKS TO KNIFE OR HANDS WHILE PEELING: Dab a tiny bit of butter or other shortening on the knife, peeler, and/or your hands, whichever it is that is troubled by sticky peels.

GREEN: The green spots on potatoes contain a natural toxin, although it generally doesn't cause any harm in small doses. If your potatoes have turned green in spots, cut away the green areas or, if you prefer, compost the potatoes entirely.

MASHED, BLAND OR TOO MUCH: There comes a time in everyone's life, often at an early age, when he or she just can't stomach another spoonful of mashed potatoes. If you have just made a large batch when this phenomenon suddenly strikes your family, try adding some nutmeg to the potatoes, forming them into patties, and frying them in butter. Not bad at all. Consider adding some cooked cabbage or kale as the Irish do and call it colcannon.

MASHED, WON'T FLUFF: Add a pinch or two of baking powder to the potatoes and keep on fluffing.

NOT ENOUGH: Now why don't you have those mashed potato flakes, as we suggested in the introduction? But enough of that. If you haven't started cooking the potatoes you do have, slice them thin and make scalloped potatoes or potatoes Anna (they're richer, so people will eat less; see a cookbook for details).

POTATO CHIPS

BROKEN: Here is something mildly interesting to do with broken potato chips—more interesting than throwing them out, at least, and faster than gluing them back together with Krazy Glue: break them up even more, and then use them as a casserole topping, to add crunch to a sandwich (tuna salad is particularly nice), or to top a salad.

SOGGY: Put them very briefly under the broiler; don't let them brown. Or you can microwave them for 30 to 60 seconds on the high setting and let them stand for 3 minutes.

POULTRY

BLAND: Try rubbing the bird with marjoram (which is also interesting in chicken salad). Mix oregano with olive oil, and rub it on the fowl. Likewise with rosemary or tarragon or thyme. Mix some hot mustard, oregano, paprika, or sesame seeds in with the batter for fried chicken. Crush three or four juniper berries into the chicken salad. And so on.

BREADING FALLS OFF: See "BREADING, Falls Off."

DIFFICULT TO CUT: Often, scissors are easier to use than knives when cutting cooked or raw birds. With cooked chicken or turkey, scissors don't shred the meat as much as a knife.

DRY: Slice your bird and arrange it on a heatproof platter. Make a sauce using equal amounts of butter and chicken broth. Pour it on the sliced bird and let it stand in a 250°F oven for 10 minutes to soak up the juices.

FEATHERY: In our modern age of convenience, most birds come defeathered. In our modern age of deteriorating personal services, often the defeathering isn't good enough. If you don't have a chicken plucker on your household staff, here are two reasonably simple methods of defeathering a fowl:

1. The hot wax treatment: Add paraffin or old candles to boiling water. Wait until the wax melts. Dip the bird up and down in the pot until it is coated with wax. Wrap in newspapers and let cool. Now, as you peel off the wax, the feathers should come off along with it. (If you can't get the wax off, stick a wick in the bird's beak and you have an emergency candle.)

2. The soap method: Heat a big pot of water to boiling. Add $1/4$ cup dishwasher detergent. Drop the fowl in the water, slosh it around for 2 or 3 minutes, and then roll it up in a towel. You should be able to rub off any remaining feathers. Follow with a cool-water rinse, and don't worry about the taste: no soap.

FREEZER BURN: Dry spots on frozen fowl can and usually do mean freezer burn. Smell the creature carefully, and if you have any doubts as to its condition, return it or junk it. If it smells okay, rub the skin with oil just before roasting.

FROZEN: Manufacturers usually recommend that frozen chickens and turkeys be defrosted slowly in the refrigerator—a process that often takes 3 or 4 days. The main reason for this recommendation is that faster thawing causes the bird to lose juices and thus becomes tougher. Also, some methods of quick thawing can raise the risk of salmonella. If you're in a hurry, put the frozen fowl in a plastic bag and place in a bowl of cold water to thaw.

GAMY: Sometimes duck or pheasant or even turkey will taste too gamy for your palate. This is no reflection on the bird's behavior in the barnyard. Ginger, sherry, and brandy (the latter two applied to the bird, please) have a tendency to lessen gamy taste in poultry. You can also rub $1/2$ teaspoon powdered ginger into the bird's skin before roasting or add any of the three to the gravy or sauce you serve over the meat.

NOT ENOUGH: Serve the poultry on a waffle that you have made by adding 2 teaspoons poultry seasoning to the dry ingredients before adding the liquid. You can get away with about half as much meat this way.

PALE: Applying paprika liberally to the skin of a fowl before roasting it will ensure a rich color. You can sprinkle it on at any point in the cooking process to help a pallid bird.

TOUGH: Meat tenderizer will work on fowl as well. For poultry cooked in liquid, try adding a pinch of baking soda to the liquid. And for broiling or roasting, tenderize the birds by rubbing them inside and out with lemon juice before cooking.

PRUNES

BLAND: Add thin lemon slices while cooking cooked prunes.

DRY, TOUGH: Cover them with boiling water and put them in the refrigerator overnight. This doesn't cook them; it just plumps them up nicely. You can do this quickly in a microwave oven. Cover a layer of prunes with water, add a squeeze of lemon juice if you wish, and cook on high for 5 minutes. Let stand for 5 minutes before either eating or refrigerating in the liquid.

PUDDINGS AND CUSTARDS

BLAND: Toss a bay leaf or a pinch of ginger into almost any kind of custard. Bland puddings can benefit from the addition of ground allspice, cinnamon, ginger, mace (especially in chocolate), and nutmeg.

BURNED: Stop stirring. Pour off the pudding or custard into a new pot, leaving the burned part at the bottom. Taste to make sure you haven't transferred the burned flavor and keep cooking—carefully this time, with much stirring.

COLD: Hot puddings and custards can be reheated without cooking them more by covering them with lettuce leaves and returning to a warm oven until you are ready for them.

CURDLING: When custard starts to curdle, the first thing to do is to stop it from cooking any further. Do this by hastily putting the pan in cold water—better still, ice water. Then beat it with an eggbeater or whisk until it is smooth again.

If the custard has already curdled, you can frequently uncurdle it with this time-consuming method: Add 1 tablespoon custard to 1 teaspoon milk or liqueur. Beat until creamy. Add the remaining custard 1 tablespoon at a time, beating each time until creamy. Then return to your recipe. You can also put your custard through a sieve or try blending it. It may end up thinner than you had planned, however, and thus become a custard sauce.

SEPARATING (BAKED CUSTARDS): This is caused by too much heat. The oven should be set at 325°F, and the custard should be in Marie's bath (that is to say, a bain-marie, with the custard dish standing in a pan of water).

SKIN IS FORMING (PUDDINGS): If the taste is compatible, sprinkle 1 teaspoon sugar on the surface. If it is not, put waxed paper on the surface and remove it when the pudding has cooled.

TOO THIN: If it's a pudding, did it reach a full boil? It needs to in order for the starch to thicken it. If it has and it's still too thin, for a creamy pudding, add one (not all) of the following for each cup of milk used: 3 tablespoons flour, 1 tablespoon cornstarch, $1^{1}/_{2}$ tablespoons rice flour,

1 tablespoon arrowroot, or 1 tablespoon tapioca. For molded puddings, add any of the following for each cup of milk used: 4 tablespoons flour, $1^{1}/_{2}$ tablespoons cornstarch, $2^{1}/_{2}$ tablespoons cornmeal, or 2 tablespoons rice flour. Mix the thickeners with a little cold milk before adding them, and be sure to bring the pudding to a boil.

For soft custard, add 1 beaten egg (or 2 yolks or 2 whites) for each cup of milk.

For molded custard, first make sure it has had plenty of time to cool, since custards thicken as they cool. If your custard is cool and still too thin, you have just created a base for a wonderful ice cream.

PUFF PASTRY

CRACKED: Cracks in baked puff pastry are often the result of dried-out dough. This time, resort to covering cracks with gravy or mustard sauce, or berry or chocolate sauce, depending on the recipe, of course. Or, use a garnish or edible decoration. Next time, make sure you keep the dough covered tightly with plastic wrap right up until the moment you're ready to bake it.

NOT SUFFICIENTLY RISEN: The pastry will still taste fine, though it won't be quite as light and flaky as it should be. Next time, make sure you use a light hand to roll out the dough. Also, for the best rise, try this trick: put the pastry into a 425°F oven, then immediately turn down the temperature to 400°F or 375°F and continue baking.

SHRUNKEN: The pastry will taste, if not look, good. Depending on degree of shrinkage, you may wish to resort to covering it with a sauce (see "Cracked," above). Next time, prior to baking, let your dough rest in the refrigerator long enough to allow the gluten to relax (overnight is best for homemade puff pastry).

PUMPKINS: *see* SQUASHES, SWEET POTATOES, PUMPKINS

PUNCH: *see* ALCOHOL

QUICHE

SOGGY CRUST: The main cause is using wet vegetables, either ones you forgot to drain or those that hold a lot of moisture (liked zucchini). Remove the portion above the crust and serve that alone. Most people either 1) won't notice, 2) will be too polite to comment, or 3) will assume it was intentional. Yes, if you have time, you can bake a round of crust and put the quiche filling on top of it. Scallop the edges so it looks intentional. How do you get the quiche out of the pan and onto the crust? Loosen it around the edge with a sharp knife. Put plastic wrap on the top of the cooled quiche. Put a kitchen towel over that. Put a plate over that. Turn it upside down. Hope.

Next time you make a quiche, you can bake the crust for 10 minutes alone before adding the filling. Or bake the quiche either on the bottom of your oven or on a pizza stone.

QUINOA

BITTER: Quinoa has a natural outer coating that has a bitter taste. Often this coating is removed before the quinoa is packaged. But if it hasn't been (or you don't know if it has), soak your quinoa in water for 30 minutes and rinse prior to cooking. If you don't have that much time, soak it for at least 5 minutes in hot water and rinse. If your quinoa is already cooked and bitter, you'll just have to judge whether it's too bitter to serve. You can always mix it with another grain to cut the taste (rice or barley or couscous—yes, we know couscous isn't a grain). Or serve it with some arugula. Then people will expect it to be somewhat bitter.

RABBIT, WELSH: *see* CHEESE, Cooked Cheese that Is
Rubbery, Tough, Stringy

RADISHES

BITTER: Roasting makes radishes sweeter. Toss them with oil and roast
at 425°F for 30 to 45 minutes, or until tender and starting to brown.

TOO MANY: See "Bitter," above, for a fine suggestion on how to use up
some of your radishes.

WILTED, SOFT, SOGGY: Soak them in ice water for 2 to 3 hours. If you
like, add 1 tablespoon vinegar or the juice of one lemon to the water.

RAGOUT: *see* STEWS

RAISINS

SHRIVELED: You can replumpify shriveled raisins by simmering them
for 3 to 4 minutes in just enough water to cover them. Or arrange
them in a thin layer in a dish, barely cover them with water, and cook
on high in a microwave for 5 minutes. Let stand for an additional
5 minutes. Use rum or sherry for some of the water if you wish. But
wait, aren't raisins *supposed* to be shriveled, though? Oh, well.

SINK TO THE BOTTOM: If the raisins are sinking to the bottom of your
cakes or cookies or whatever, coat them lightly with flour and they will
disperse themselves throughout the whatever, just the way you wanted.
If what you are making is raisin upside-down cake, ignore this.

STUCK TOGETHER: Heat your congealed mass of raisins in the oven at
300°F for a few minutes and they will unstick themselves.

RASPBERRIES: *see* BERRIES

RHUBARB

TOO TART: All rhubarb is too tart, some of us think. To detart it without adding absurd amounts of sugar, cut up the rhubarb and soak it for 3 minutes in hot water to which you have added a pinch of either baking soda or salt.

RICE

BOILING OVER: First, blow on the surface of the water. This will cool the water down enough so that it will stop boiling over. For a longer-term preventive, toss a lump of butter in the pot; it will flavor the rice pleasantly as well.

BURNED: As soon as you discover you've burned the rice again, turn off the flame, place the heel of a loaf of bread on top of the rice, cover the pot, and wait for 5 minutes. Virtually all the scorched taste should disappear into the bread. Serve the rice to friends and the bread to enemies.

COLD: If you're one of the few people around who doesn't have a microwave, reheat your rice without overcooking it by putting it in either a big sieve or a colander and placing it over a pan of boiling or simmering water (depending on how cold it is and how fast you need it). Keep the rice from touching the water.

NOT WHITE ENOUGH: Are you sure it isn't brown rice? All right, just asking. Add 1 teaspoon lemon juice to the cooking water and the rice will turn a shade whiter.

TOO MUCH: You can reheat leftover rice (see "Cold," above), add it to soup, use it as a casserole ingredient, or combine it with custard to make a rice pudding. Or you could make something unusual, like the following dish.

Rice Fritters

½ package dry yeast
½ cup very warm water
  (about 110°F)
1½ to 2 cups leftover
  lukewarm rice
3 eggs, beaten
1 cup all-purpose flour

¼ cup granulated sugar
½ teaspoon salt
¼ teaspoon cinnamon
Oil for deep-frying
Confectioners' sugar
  (optional)
Whipped cream (optional)

Dissolve the yeast in the water in a large bowl. Stir in the rice. Cover and let sit overnight in the refrigerator. The next day, add the eggs, flour, granulated sugar, salt, and cinnamon; stir well and let it sit for another hour or so, this time at room temperature. Drop this mixture, one teaspoonful at a time, into oil heated to 360°F and fry until golden brown. Serve as an accompaniment to ham or chicken, or sprinkle with confectioners' sugar and serve with whipped cream for a dessert.

UNEVEN COOKING: When the rice at the bottom of the pot is cooked and the top of the pot is raw, it means too much steam is escaping. Give the rice a big stir, cover the pot either with foil or with a bath towel (be sure to fold the loose ends up over the top), replace the lid, and keep right on cooking.

ROAST BEEF

DIFFICULT TO CARVE: Let the roast sit for 15 minutes once you have removed it from the oven. The juices will redistribute themselves and the roast will be less likely to fall apart as you carve it.

NOT BROWNING: Steam impedes browning. If the roast is covered, there will be more steam, so leave it uncovered. It is generally best to roast meat in a shallow pan.

NOT ENOUGH: Slice the beef thin, serve it over toast, and cover with a sauce. You can use cheese sauce, tomato sauce, or hollandaise (you *have* completed your culinary first aid kit by now, haven't you?), or add a pinch of tarragon to hollandaise and use the resulting béarnaise sauce.

OVERCOOKED: Cut off all unusable burned pieces and slice the roast thin. It will probably be dry and tough, in which case you can float it in a sauce (see "Not Enough," above).

TOO RARE: Often the outside slices of a roast are acceptable when the middle section is too rare for some people, misguided as they may be. Serve the outer slices and return the rest to cook while you eat the first helpings, or broil the too-rare slices to the desired doneness.

TOO TOUGH: Unfortunately, this is usually discovered at the dinner table, when all you can do is slice it very thin. But you'll probably have leftovers. The good news is that the meat cooked by a dry method (roasting or broiling, for example) can be tenderized by a moist-heat method for its second appearance. Braising and stewing, which use low heat for a long cooking time, are best. Consider, then, resurrecting your roast as an impressive beef bourguignon.

ROLLS: *see* BREAD AND ROLLS

RUM: *see* ALCOHOL

RUTABAGAS

SMELLY: A recent national survey showed that .0000000001 percent of the population is troubled by smelly rutabagas. For you, madam or sir, this advice: add 1 teaspoon sugar to the cooking water.

SALAD: *see* GREENS

SALAD DRESSING: *see also* SAUCES

BLAND: One way to pep up bottles of store-bought French or Italian dressing is to put a halved clove of garlic in the bottle and let it stand overnight or longer.

TOO ACIDIC: Add a small pinch of baking soda or sugar.

SALSIFY

DARKENING: The same person who has smelly rutabagas also has darkening salsify. Store this herb in water to which you have added 2 tablespoons vinegar or the juice of 1 lemon for each quart of water.

SALT, PEPPER

CLOGGED SHAKER: Salt shakers clog when the salt becomes moist. You can overcome this problem by putting $1/2$ teaspoon raw rice or a tiny bit of blotter paper into the salt shaker. Or mix about 1 tablespoon cornstarch into a normal-sized box of salt; it will pour freely.

Put about $1/2$ teaspoon whole peppercorns into a pepper shaker and not only will it keep the pepper pouring, it will also impart a lovely fresh-pepper smell, if your nose can detect that sort of thing.

HAVE ONE KIND, NEED ANOTHER: For most cooking you can substitute kosher and table salt for each other. It's generally recommended to use $1^1/_4$ to $1^1/_2$ teaspoons kosher salt for every 1 teaspoon table salt. Sea salt can also be substituted. However, how finely or coarsely it's ground will, of course, affect its measurement. Table salt is generally not recommended for pickling or canning because it usually has anticaking agents. These aren't harmful, but they are not water-soluble and will collect on the bottom of your jar and look a bit odd. Either kosher or pickling salt should be used. (And pickling salt can be used in any other cooking as well, although, of course, it is more likely to cake.)

Black and white pepper can be substituted for each other. Black pepper has a slightly stronger flavor, but most sources recommend substituting equal amounts. Obviously, if you're adding to taste, you might want to use a bit less black pepper to begin with.

SALT PORK: *see* PORK

SANDWICHES: *see* BREAD AND ROLLS; MUFFINS; *specific sandwich ingredients*

SAUCES

BITTER: A common cause of an unexpectedly bitter sauce is tomato seeds. This time, strain them out as best you can. (Then, if necessary, see "Too Thin," below.) Next time, see "TOMATOES, Seedy."

BLAND: Every herb, spice, seasoning, bottled flavoring, and kind of cooking alcohol in your house can be used in sauces. There is no excuse whatsoever for a flat or bland sauce. Consult your favorite cookbook and get to work. (If you are reducing a sauce, add seasonings at the end or you may overdo it, since the herbs don't reduce.) If you absolutely can't think of anything else to do, add a dollop of sherry to any sauce you're preparing, and at least people will know you tried. See "Hollandaise Sauce," under "First Aid Supplies," for simple instructions for converting this store-bought, ready-to-use product into quick béarnaise, Choron, and Maltaise sauces.

CATSUP: See "Ketchup Won't Pour," below.

CURDLED: Remove the sauce from the heat at once. For delicate sauces like hollandaise, add an ice cube to retard further cooking. Beat hard with a hand beater or whisk (having removed the ice cube). If necessary, strain the sauce, too. For other sauces, try adding a little cream, then continue cooking. Next time, use a double boiler or lower heat, stir constantly, and add the fragile curdle-producing ingredients (usually eggs, cream, or sour cream) at room temperature just before serving.

FATTY: Chill, skim off the fat, and reheat. For fast skimming, remove as much fat as you can with a spoon (it's easier if you tilt the pot). Then toss in a few ice cubes, wait until the fat congeals around them, and remove them. Blot the last bits up with paper towels laid on the surface of the sauce and reheat.

Consider a sauce boat or pitcher in which the spout goes to the bottom, so you are pouring the least fatty sauce directly from the bottom. Most gourmet or kitchen stores stock such things.

KETCHUP WON'T POUR: Put a soda straw down to the bottom of the bottle. It will transmit enough air down to the bottom to permit the ketchup to pour readily.

LUMPY: If you can, push the sauce through a strainer. If you can't, beat it with a whisk or hand beater. Use electric appliances (beater, blender, or food processor) only as a last resort.

NOT ENOUGH: Whether your problem is too little liquid in a stew or not enough gravy for a roast, the solution is basically the same: Add more liquid to what you have (though don't try to add more than an amount of liquid equal to what you started out with), reseason, decide if you can get away with a thinner sauce, and then thicken if you must. Consider using something more substantial than water for your thinning: consommé or bouillon (be careful with the salt when you reseason), liquid from a compatible cooked vegetable you're serving with the meal, or even orange juice for something like ham or poultry-based dishes. To avoid slowing everything down, have your liquid hot before adding it.

Cream sauces can be extended by adding more white sauce (you'll find white sauce recipes in most cookbooks) or even cream of mushroom or cream of chicken soup if you're really strapped for time.

Hollandaise-based sauces are best left in their original, rich, unadulterated state. Put food and sauce on plates in the kitchen yourself; no one will even think to question the volume of the sauce.

NOT RICH ENOUGH: Add heavy cream, 1 teaspoon at a time, after the sauce is cooked and removed from the heat. A lump of butter, applied in like manner, will also work.

NOT SMOOTH ENOUGH: A little butter stirred into a cream sauce before serving will produce a more satiny texture.

SALTY: The only certain cure for saltiness is to increase the volume without adding more salt. Otherwise, you can add a couple of pinches of brown sugar. It tends to overcome saltiness without adding noticeable sweetness. You can also try adding a squeeze of lemon juice to balance the saltiness.

SEPARATED: See "Curdled," above.

TOO THIN: There are almost as many thickeners as there are sauces. The universal one is time. Keep cooking until some of the liquid evaporates and the sauce will inevitably thicken. (Some French recipes require sauce ingredients to be reduced by 90 percent or more. There is an account of a famous sauce whose secret recipe began "Reduce 1 ox to 1 cup.")

Cornstarch is a good thickener when translucency of sauce is desirable, as in many dessert or Chinese sauces. Add 1 tablespoon per $1^1/_2$ to 2 cups of cooking liquid. To prevent lumps, dissolve the cornstarch in cold water before adding it to the hot sauce and bringing the sauce to a boil.

To use arrowroot, add $1^1/_2$ teaspoons per $1^1/_2$ to 2 cups of liquid, but only when the sauce will be served within 10 minutes. To prevent lumps, dissolve the arrowroot in cold water before adding it to the hot sauce and bringing the sauce to a boil.

One cup of milk or a milk-based sauce will be thickened by 2 tablespoons flour, 3 to 4 tablespoons tapioca, or 2 egg yolks beaten with $^1/_4$ cup cream or evaporated milk. The latter should be done only in the top of a double boiler, stirring constantly. Bread crumbs can be used (as in the classic British bread sauce), but they will change the texture of the sauce somewhat. Start with $^1/_4$ cup, though some recipes will use as much as an entire cup.

Other sauce thickeners that may be appropriate for your particular sauce are rice, barley, milk, cream, puréed vegetables, and mashed potato flakes.

SAUERKRAUT

TOO STRONG: Some of us prefer it that way. For those of you who don't, a good rinse is in order. Or simmer it with brown sugar ($^1/_4$ cup per pound of sauerkraut) for 30 minutes or more, adding liquid as needed (water or light beer is good).

SAUSAGES

BURSTING, SPLITTING, EXPLODING, ETC.: There are two schools of thought: the Low Temperaturists and the Skin Piercers. Either is likely to work; both are unnecessary. Next time, cook the sausages at a gentle simmer using just enough water to cover.

SCALLIONS: *see* ONIONS

SEAFOOD: *see* FISH AND SEAFOOD

SEASONINGS: *see* HERBS, SPICES

SEITAN

BLAND: The most basic recipe for homemade seitan calls for gluten flour (also known as vital wheat gluten) and liquid. For more flavor, you can add nutritional yeast, sage, thyme, garlic, broth, soy sauce, and tomato paste or ketchup. If you've already cooked up some bland seitan or if the stuff you bought from the store is tasteless, you'll just have to make an extra-flavorful sauce for it.

BREADY: You probably needed more high-gluten flour and/or less liquid. Also, when simmering your seitan next time, make sure that you start with cold liquid and never let the liquid fully boil. For now, you may want to take your bready seitan, slice it, and brown it in a pan. This will help disguise the texture somewhat.

RUBBERY: You may have used too much high-gluten flour. It's a necessary ingredient to hold the seitan together, but it can cause rubberiness. Use a 1:4 ratio of another flour (we recommend chickpea, though all-purpose is fine) to gluten flour to avoid this. You may also need more liquid in your seitan. And when cooking, be sure it's fully submerged in liquid (if you're simmering it) and that you cook it long enough. But what to do now with your rubbery seitan? Your best option is to cut it into small pieces and brown them. Serve with a sauce or in a pot pie.

SPONGY: Have you let it cool completely? Seitan firms up as it cools. If you have, use the same fix as for rubbery seitan. It won't be perfect, but it will certainly be edible.

SHORTENING: *see* FAT, LARD, SHORTENING

SHRIMP: *see* FISH AND SEAFOOD

SODA POP

DECARBONATED: Cover tightly and shake well; some of the carbonation will be restored if it isn't too far gone. Open carefully; the soda may shoot across the room if you do it too fast.

UNINSPIRED: When you have grown weary of all the usual flavors, it is fun to start experimenting with combining two kinds of soda (cherry and cola is, of course, a classic, but many others make sense, too: ginger ale with orange or grape; cream soda with strawberry or cherry; cola with lemon or lime). Our family adds flavoring agents (essence of cherry, rum, almond, peppermint, and the like) to various sodas (cream soda with almond is a special favorite). Milk also does interesting things, as in the classic "root beer cow" (about one-third milk and two-thirds root beer), the chocolate egg cream (no egg or cream; just cream soda, milk, and chocolate essence or syrup), and so forth.

SOUFFLÉS

DOESN'T RISE (OR RISES, THEN SINKS DURING BAKING): It probably still tastes good (perhaps even better; a collapsed chocolate soufflé we created while doing research for this book was wonderfully dense and chocolatey). To disguise a sunken savory (nonsweet) soufflé, remove it from the pan, cover with cheese, and broil. Call it a frittata. Or simply cover it with a sauce appropriate to the ingredients. A sweet soufflé can be covered with whipped cream or a sauce.

Traditional soufflés won't rise again if reheated. Some cookbooks offer recipes for "double-rising" soufflés that do, in fact, rise again when reheated. We're not using up three pages to present these, because we feel it is more a matter of the ego than the palate.

Next time, be sure to bake the soufflé on the lowest rack in the oven. This is partly because it is hotter down there (in most ovens), and partly so that, as it does rise, it won't smash into the top of the oven, quite possibly lifting the roof off your house.

TOP IS BROWNING TOO FAST: Make a foil "lid" to cover it. You'll have to guess the approximate size because you shouldn't take the soufflé out of the oven while it's baking. Cut a circle about 2 inches wider than the top of the soufflé. Bend the edges up about 1 inch in from the outside (to make a pie tin–like shape). Oil the inside lightly. Open the oven and quickly slide the foil, oiled side down, onto the soufflé and continue baking.

UNCROWNED: To make a crown, just before baking, run a knife around the mixture about 1 inch from the edge. The tip of the knife should be near but not at the bottom of the pan.

SOUPS

BLAND: Bouillons and extracts of beef or chicken are a mainstay here. For vegetarians, widely available vegetable bouillon is an excellent flavoring. But consider also yeast extracts like Marmite. Following is a list of common herbs and spices and some of their best uses in soups. You can use fresh herbs if you have them, but dried herbs are fine, too.

allspice (whole): pea, ham, vegetable, beef, and tomato soups
    (remove allspice berries before serving)
basil: tomato, turtle, and spinach soups and minestrone
    ($^1/_2$ teaspoon per 4 servings)
bay leaf: vegetable and tomato soups and minestrone
chervil: tomato and spinach soups
cumin: a dash in creamed chicken, fish, and pea soups
juniper berries: use about 1 per serving in vegetable, beef, lamb,
    and oxtail soups
mace: 1 or 2 blades (or pinches, if it's ground) in 4 cups of
    consommé stock
marjoram: spinach, clam, turtle, and onion soups ($^1/_2$ teaspoon
    per 4 servings)
oregano: tomato, bean, corn, and pea soups

paprika (hot): in modest quantities for tomato, bean, and pea soups

rosemary: chicken, pea, spinach, potato, and fish soups

sage: creamed soups and chowders

savory: fish, consommé, lentil, bean, tomato, and vegetable soups

sesame seed: creamed soups (sprinkle on before serving)

tarragon: tomato, vegetable, and seafood soups

thyme: chicken, onion, potato, tomato, and seafood soups, gumbo, and borscht (stir in $1/2$ teaspoon 10 minutes before serving)

Also consider leaving the soup alone and putting something interesting in the bowls, such as flavored croutons, a dollop of sour cream, crème fraîche (see "CRÈME FRAÎCHE"), decorative swirls of tomato paste, sherry, or curry powder. See also "Not Enough," below.

BOUILLON CLOUDY: Add eggshells. Please remove them before serving. Or add egg whites. To remove them (if you want to), strain through a cheesecloth-lined strainer or colander.

FATTY OR GREASY: If you have the time, refrigerate the soup. The fat will solidify on the top. Remove it and reheat the soup.

You can float a grease collector on the top. Lettuce leaves, blotting paper, and paper towels all make good grease collectors.

Another fast technique is to make a "grease magnet" by wrapping a few ice cubes in a terry cloth towel. Run this over the surface of the soup and the fat will cling to it. A ladleful of ice cubes will have the same effect.

LIGHT: Commercial soup colorings are available, but some people think they have a telltale aroma. Depending on the kind of soup, you can darken it using tomato skins, tomato paste, soy sauce (taste to make sure you're not oversalting it, though), or even food coloring. In fact, if you're overly concerned about your soup being too light, you may want to keep a supply of brown icing color, which is available as a gel or a paste in stores that stock a good selection of baking supplies.

You can also try adding a tablespoon of caramelized sugar. This works well with soups that feature cabbage. If you think you've overdone it and can detect a sweet taste, add a tablespoon or two of vinegar. The result will be a much more complex and interestingly flavored soup.

NOT ENOUGH: Rather than adding more liquid, consider making it spicier, thus servable in smaller portions. Use, for example, hot sauce or taco sauce in tomato- or chicken-based soups; aioli (garlic mayonnaise) in fishy soups; or curry powder in many soups. Also consider making it richer for the same reason, adding, for instance, a roux and heavy cream.

SALTY: The surest solution is to increase the quantity of the liquid without increasing the quantity of the salt. But if this isn't practical, try one of the following techniques:

1. Add tomatoes. If it is the right kind of soup, add a can of tomatoes. They are sufficiently bland to use up a lot of the saltiness.

2. Add a few pinches of brown sugar. It won't desalt the soup, but it may help cover up the salty taste without sweetening the soup.

3. Add a squeeze of lemon juice, which can counteract saltiness.

4. Use potatoes. Add a thinly sliced raw potato to the soup, leaving it in until the slices become translucent. The potato may absorb some of the salt from the liquid.

There are skeptics who ask, "If it is possible to remove the salt from liquid easily, why aren't we desalting the oceans?" To this we reply, "Because it would require 488,391,000,000,000 tons of sliced potatoes."

TOO MUCH: Contrary to almost everyone else's opinion, leftover soup can be kept quite a long time without freezing it, if you're willing to work at it. Almost any soup will keep in a covered pot in the refrigerator for a week. If you have a great soup that you want to keep for longer but don't want to freeze, take it out of the refrigerator and heat it to boiling every couple of days; it will last even longer. But if it's really that great, why aren't you eating it?

TOO THIN: First, see the section on "SAUCES, Too Thin" for several useful hints. Thickeners peculiar to soups include these:

Mashed potatoes or potato flakes (which also have a tendency to absorb seasonings, so check for taste after adding).

Some of the soup's own ingredients (e.g., vegetables, beans, or lentils) ground up in a blender or food processor. (These should be additional ingredients, but in a pinch may be filched from the soup.)

A mixture of $^1/_2$ cup cornstarch and $^1/_4$ cup sherry, stirred in shortly before serving.

For each original cup of liquid, 1 teaspoon barley or rice or 2 teaspoons flour (first dissolved in enough cold water to make a runny mixture, then stirred into the soup) stirred in during the last hour of cooking.

One egg yolk beaten with 1 tablespoon cream or sherry, mixed with a small amount of hot soup, and then stirred into the rest just before serving.

Stale bread (especially if you can float a heaping tablespoon of Parmesan cheese on top, too).

For long-cooking soups, a handful of oatmeal or barley flakes.

For pea and bean soups, 1 teaspoon vinegar. (It will thicken the soup without affecting the taste.)

SOUP STOCK

NEED SOME, HAVE NONE: Two bouillon cubes (beef, chicken, or vegetable) in 1 cup water make an acceptable substitute for beef, chicken, or vegetable stock. Watch your salt levels, though, since bouillon is saltier than stock. But if you have no bouillon either, some soups work fine using water, provided that you up the seasonings. Consider adding a splash of soy sauce, a dollop of white wine or sherry, and a bit of garlic if you haven't already.

SOUR CREAM

NEED SOME, HAVE NONE: For cooking purposes, not topping purposes, add 1 tablespoon mild vinegar or lemon juice to 1 cup of evaporated milk.

For topping purposes, not cooking purposes, put cottage cheese in a blender or food processor, sweeten it to taste, and if it doesn't taste right, add a tiny bit of vanilla extract.

Or make crème fraîche (see, surprisingly, "CRÈME FRAÎCHE").

SPAGHETTI: *see* PASTA

SPAGHETTI SAUCE: *see* SAUCES

SPICES: *see* HERBS, SPICES

SPINACH: *see* GREENS

SQUASHES, SWEET POTATOES, PUMPKINS

BLAND: Squash has a luscious affinity for ginger. To taste this your-self, serve squash of almost any sort with 1 heaping tablespoon ginger marmalade per serving. If you don't have ginger marmalade, orange marmalade is nice instead. But back to ginger. You can also purée your winter squash with some grated fresh or powdered ginger. Add a little brown sugar, too.

If this doesn't suit your fancy, try basil, ground cloves, dill seed, dill weed, mace, marjoram, oregano, sage, or thyme. Sweet potato is also marvelous with a spoonful of almond butter stirred in. No almond butter? Peanut butter is almost as good.

DIFFICULT TO CUT: Winter squash can be rock hard. To make cutting squash easier, place it on the floor of a microwave oven and heat on high for 2 minutes. Let it stand for 2 minutes before cutting.

NOT ENOUGH: Orange-colored squashes go well with fruits, so combine chunks, or even purées, of them with sautéed apples or pears or sec-tions of mandarin or regular oranges.

Green and yellow squashes love tomatoes.

STRINGY: Beat stringy cooked squash with an electric mixer at high speed for 10 seconds, then at low speed for 60 seconds. Wash the strings off the beater (the floor, the walls, the dog), and repeat if necessary and possible. Or just run it through a food processor.

TOO MUCH: Squash keeps better than almost any other vegetable, so don't worry.

WATERY: This a common pumpkin problem. Did you cook the Halloween jack-o'-lantern? That type of pumpkin tends to be very watery (and often bland; see "Bland," above). Leave the cooked pumpkin in a strainer set over a bowl for several hours (or, better yet, overnight in the refrigerator) to allow the excess water to drain off.

SQUID

TOUGH: Generally, squid is cooked very quickly or for a long time. Somewhere in the middle, it becomes chewy. (We liken eating tough squid to chewing on a pencil eraser.) So most likely you're in that middle area and should keep cooking. Cooking it in liquid is best.

STEAK

BREADING FALLS OFF: If this is your problem with chicken-fried steak, see "BREADING, Falls Off."

CURLING: Cut through the fat along the edge of the meat every inch or so and turn it over. You can turn it back again later.

OVERDONE: Continue cooking until it is completely charred and use it to scratch pictures on the walls of your cave. Or, perhaps more realistically, cut it into small chunks and use it in a pot of chili.

Or how about covering your mistake (and the steak) with the following sauce?

Hot Sauce for Steak

FOR ABOUT 2 POUNDS OF STEAK

$2/3$ cup chopped onions
$1/3$ cup chopped green bell
   peppers
2 tablespoons olive oil
$2/3$ cup diced tomatoes
1 teaspoon salt

$1/8$ teaspoon chile powder
$1/2$ teaspoon paprika
$2/3$ cup ground peanuts
1 cup chicken broth
$1/4$ cup sour or heavy cream

Sauté the onions and peppers in the olive oil for 5 minutes in a saucepan over medium heat. Add the tomatoes, salt, chile powder, and paprika and sauté for 5 minutes. Stir in the peanuts and broth and simmer for 30 minutes. Stir in the cream, pour over your steak, and serve.

TOUGH: If you don't have or would rather not use tenderizer, and if perforating the steak with the tines of a fork every $1/4$ inch doesn't appeal, try pounding it all over with the edge of a metal pie plate. Very effective, especially if you remove the pie first.

STEWS

BLAND: No stew has been made that couldn't be perked up by adding $1/4$ cup sherry and stirring well just before serving. (If you think you've made one that couldn't be so improved, we'd like to see it. Smear some on a postcard and send it on in.) If sherry doesn't work for you, try black pepper, hot paprika, Worcestershire sauce, or black bean sauce.

BURNED: Transfer the unstuck part, without scraping any of the stuck part, to another pot at once. Using a wooden spoon is best. Add more water if necessary. Add some more onions; they tend to overcome any of the burned flavor that may remain.

FALLING APART: Sometimes stew just cooks itself to bits. You can't reassemble it, so serve it over noodles or rice; it will look like a great sauce.

FATTY: If the consistency permits, the fat may be skimmed off with a paper towel. If it doesn't, chill the stew after it is fully cooked (you can put it in the freezer for a while) and then remove the solidified fat. Most stews taste better the next day anyway.

NOT ENOUGH: Serve the stew over noodles. Add more vegetables—and don't forget that beans are protein food. A can of kidney or lima beans can stretch a stew without thinning it out.

SALTY: Increase the quantity without adding more salt if at all possible. If not, add a couple of pinches of brown sugar; it tends to mask the saltiness without adding any noticeable sweetness.

TOO THIN: The best thickener for most stews is a handful of potato flakes stirred in. See "SOUPS, Too Thin," for additional suggestions.

TOUGH: This usually means that you haven't cooked it long enough. How much time have you? You can fish the chunks of meat out and cut them smaller. A tablespoon of vinegar added to the pot will also help make tough stew meat tender. The acid in tomatoes has the same effect, so add some fresh or canned tomatoes if they will be compatible.

TURNING GRAY: If, when you're browning the meat before assembling the stew, it's turning gray instead of brown, the problem is too much moisture in the pan, which causes the meat to steam. This time, try to eliminate the overcrowding, either by removing some of the meat or using a larger pan. Next time, be sure the meat is very dry before browning.

STOCK: *see* SOUPS

STRAWBERRIES: *see* BERRIES

STRING BEANS: *see* BEANS, LIMA AND GREEN

STUFFING

BLAND: Add allspice, basil, a crushed bay leaf, coriander, ginger, marjoram, oregano, sage, savory, and/or thyme.

Or perhaps the stuffing could use diced celery, chopped chestnuts or walnuts, diced onions (browned or not), or bacon, browned and crumbled in.

SUGAR

HARD, LUMPY, SOLIDIFIED: Here are seven things to do with hardened or lumpy sugar—the least drastic first, and so on, up to the last resort.

1. Push it through a sieve.
2. Roll it out with a rolling pin.
3. Steam it in the top of a double boiler. (This works well for brown sugar only.)
4. Put it in its bag (but not a box) in a 350°F oven. By the time the bag is warm, the sugar should be softened or delumped.
5. Put it through a food processor, blender, or meat grinder.
6. Put a wedge of apple into the box or bag of sugar and reclose it. Microwave it on high for 20 seconds per cup of sugar. Let it stand for 5 minutes. Repeat if necessary.
7. Give up and melt it down over low heat on the stove. It makes good syrup. Add extracts, such as vanilla, maple, or butterscotch.

To keep sugar, especially brown sugar, from going hard or lumpy in the future, keep it in an airtight jar, preferably in the refrigerator. To be doubly sure, keep a piece bread in the jar.

NEED SOME, HAVE NONE (GRANULATED SUGAR): In baking, the following may be substituted for 1 cup of sugar: use $^3/_4$ cup honey and reduce a liquid in the recipe by $^1/_4$ cup; use $1^1/_3$ cups molasses and reduce the liquid by $^1/_3$ cup; use $1^1/_2$ cups corn syrup and reduce the liquid by $^1/_4$ cup; or use $^3/_4$ cup maple syrup and reduce the liquid by $^1/_4$ cup. And keep in mind that it will change the flavor and very possibly the texture of your recipe.

Also bear in mind that you can make superfine sugar out of regular granulated sugar by giving it a whirl in your blender or food processor.

NEED SOME, HAVE NONE (BROWN SUGAR): You can use white sugar instead of brown. For each cup of sugar, add $^1/_4$ cup molasses and decrease the liquid in the recipe by 3 tablespoons.

SWEET POTATOES: *see* SQUASHES, SWEET POTATOES, PUMPKINS

SWISS CHARD: *see* GREENS

SYRUPS

CRYSTALLIZED: Heat it gently and the crystals should go away. Probably the simplest way to do this is by standing the syrup bottle in a large bowl of hot water. Alternatively, heat the syrup for 90 seconds per cup on the high setting in a microwave oven.

TACO SHELLS

STALE: Mildly stale taco shells can be recrisped by heating them for 15 to 60 seconds in the microwave or for 6 to 8 minutes in a 300°F oven.

TAPIOCA

GLUEY: It's overcooked. And, unfortunately, it can't be unglued. (Perhaps you were planning to put up some wallpaper?) Next time, stop cooking short of the consistency you want, as it will set more as it cools.

WON'T THICKEN: Old tapioca won't thicken. If you've used it to try to thicken something like a pie filling, you'll have a loose (though still delicious) pie. If it's a pudding, you can add some arrowroot or some cooked rice and an egg and whisk constantly over low heat.

TEA

CLOUDY: For hot tea, put a couple of lemon slices in the pitcher or pot. For iced tea, add a dash of boiling water.

NEED TO SWEETEN, NO SUGAR: There are other sweeteners you can use, such as agave, honey, or corn syrup. But you knew that already. Why not try candy, like peppermint sticks, lemon drops, or cinnamon balls. Fun and tasty! If you use milk as well as sweetener, how about sweetened condensed milk—kill the milk bird and sugar bird with one can.

TEMPEH

BITTER: The flavor of tempeh can be a bit bitter, which doesn't bother some people. If it bothers you, steaming it mitigates some of the bitterness. Steam your tempeh for 10 to 15 minutes if you plan to continue cooking it in some other way afterward, and for 20 minutes if that's all the cooking it's going to get. If it's already cooked and too bitter for you, there's not much to do, but it does go well with some nice bland rice.

BLAND: Tempeh takes well to marinades and sauces with a variety of flavors, such as soy sauce, vinegar, citrus, coconut, ginger, and peanut butter.

MOLDY: What color is the mold? Tempeh is fermented and commonly has white or black veins of mold. It's fine to eat. Honest. (You wouldn't throw away your blue cheese because of a little mold, would you?) Other colors of mold, though, like green for instance, indicate that it's spoiled.

TOFU

BLAND: Some people love the delicate flavor of tofu, but others ask "what flavor?" The flavor-seeking folks are the ones who should note that tofu soaks up flavors incredibly well. Marinate it. Good ingredients to try include soy sauce, citrus, hot chiles or chile paste, rice vinegar, garlic, and sesame oil. Experiment.

WATERY OR FALLING APART: First make sure you have the right kind. Silken tofu is best for puréeing to make dressings, puddings, sauces: Don't try to cube this kind unless you're serving it cold with soy sauce or putting it in the bottom of bowls of miso soup. If you're making a stir-fry or other entrée, you should use firm or extra-firm tofu. You may also want to press the extra water out of it. Fancy tofu pressers exist, but you can just put it on a plate, put another plate on top of it, and weight it down with something like a large can. Wait for 30 minutes and then drain the water off. If you're already cooking your tofu and it's too watery, just turn up the heat and keep cooking until the water evaporates.

TOMATILLOS

NEED SOME, HAVE NONE: Green tomatoes can often be substituted. However, tomatillos are juicier and more acidic than green tomatoes, so add a squirt of lemon juice. We have been particularly successful substituting green tomatoes in an enchilada sauce.

TOMATOES

ACIDIC: Canned tomatoes sometimes get an unpleasantly acidic flavor. In this case, add 1 teaspoon sugar to a 28-ounce can. If you don't want the sweetness of added sugar, try mixing in 1 teaspoon baking soda.

BLAND: In winter, canned tomatoes will often have more taste than the "fresh" tomato-oid objects sold in supermarkets. Cooked tomatoes go nicely with basil, celery seed, ground cloves, oregano, or sage. Of course, if you're making a salad, canned tomatoes are probably not what you want. In that case, add something with zing to your dressing: good mustard, some kind of hot pepper sauce, or grated fresh onion will help.

DIFFICULT TO PEEL: Did you know that there are peelers made specifically for soft fruits and vegetables like tomatoes? They're revolutionary! But if you don't have one, pour boiling water over the tomatoes and let sit for 3 minutes. Or hold them over an open flame, skewered on a long fork, until the skin breaks. This heat treatment is permanent, so you can boil now and peel later if it suits your purpose.

If you don't want to heat the tomatoes at all, try stroking the skin with the dull edge of a kitchen knife until the skin is all wrinkled. It should come off easily at this juncture. (If it doesn't, perhaps you are at the wrong juncture.)

GREEN: Green tomatoes will ripen off the vine when wrapped in newspaper and stored in a cool place. However, they will ripen fairly slowly—at least 4 or 5 days from green to red. Wouldn't you rather make tomato pickles (see your cookbook) or perhaps the following, which are especially good with lamb?

Southern Fried Tomatoes

½ cup cornmeal
½ teaspoon dried thyme
1 tablespoon brown sugar
Green tomatoes, thickly
    sliced

Salt and pepper
Butter for frying

In a shallow bowl, mix together the cornmeal, thyme, and sugar. Sprinkle the tomato slices with salt and pepper. Dip the slices in the cornmeal mixture and fry in butter until brown.

HAVE ONE KIND, NEED ANOTHER: In cooking, 1 cup of drained canned tomatoes is equivalent to 1½ cups fresh tomatoes, chopped, then simmered for 10 minutes.

OLD: When your fresh tomatoes are getting on in days, try turning them over. Tomatoes will keep longer when stored stem side down.

SEEDY: You may wish to remove the seeds before cooking, since they can make sauces and soups bitter. Cut the tomato in half crosswise and flick the seeds out with the point of a small knife, or use a food mill to purée them and remove the seeds and skins all at once. For ripe plum tomatoes, cut off the stem end and squeeze the tomato; the seeds should come shooting out.

TOO MANY: You can use tomatoes in dozens of ways at every meal, from tomato omelettes for breakfast, to homemade Bloody Marys for a brunch (put 1 tomato, 1 shot of vodka, and 1 dash of Worcestershire sauce in a blender and blend at high speed for 1 minute), to tomato sorbet for dessert. The only important thing to remember is that tomatoes should never be frozen, as they become hopelessly mushy (at which point they're suitable for cooking only).

UNRIPE: They will ripen faster in a closed paper bag in indirect sunlight.

TOMATO SOUP: *see* SOUPS

TONGUE

BLAND: There's not a whole lot you can do with a bland tongue, but you might add four or five whole allspice berries and/or some celery to the cooking water next time. This time, know that tongue marries well with mustard (stone-ground is nice), horseradish, tomato-based sauces, sautéed onions, and sauerkraut, among other things.

DIFFICULT TO PEEL: Add 1 tablespoon vinegar to the cooking water and cook for an additional 10 minutes. Peel while the tongue is hot.

TORTILLAS

DRY: This is an issue particularly with corn tortillas. Use them to make enchiladas, not for filling and serving as tacos. If you microwave them, they will soften up temporarily. Work fast to roll them up and cover generously with sauce.

TUNA FISH: *see* FISH AND SEAFOOD

TURKEY: *see* POULTRY

TURNIPS

BLAND: So whoever heard of a lively turnip? You can try to liven yours up with either dill seed, dill weed, or poppy seeds in the cooking water, and good luck to you.

OLD: Old turnips will taste younger and better if you blanch them before cooking. To blanch a turnip, plunge it into a pot of boiling water large enough so that the boiling doesn't stop. Leave it in for 5 minutes and then proceed as you will. You can blanch your turnips in advance, dipping them in cold water after the 5 minutes to stop the cooking, and use them much later if you wish.

SMELLY: Turnips will smell a lot less if you add 1 teaspoon sugar to the cooking water.

TURNIP GREENS: *see* GREENS

There are very few foods that begin with "U." In fact, only two come to mind that are relevant to this book.

UGLI FRUIT: See "GRAPEFRUITS" for tips on peeling or serving this truly ugly cross between a grapefruit and a tangerine.

UPSIDE-DOWN CAKE

STUCK TO PAN: If the cake has cooled, heat it in the oven and it should flop out onto your waiting plate. If it's hopelessly stuck, it will make a wonderful base for a dessert. Spoon the cake into stemmed glasses or into bowls. Sprinkle it with dessert wine (if you wish) and cover the untidy cake piles with warm pudding of your choice (butterscotch or vanilla work well here) and a dollop of whipped cream. You may never flip an upside-down cake right-side up again.

VEAL

BLAND: Consider the addition of these seasonings, all of which do something for veal: allspice, celery seed (sprinkle it on a roast), chervil, cloves (five or six in the gravy), marjoram, oregano, paprika, rosemary, saffron, sage (rub the roast with it), or tarragon.

DARK: The younger the calf from which the veal comes, the lighter in color and the more tender the meat. If you suspect your veal is from an older animal (because it's dark pink rather than ivory colored) and you wanted white meat, soak the veal overnight in milk in the refrigerator. If you don't have time to do that, you can blanch it briefly to make it look younger.

VEGETABLES: *see specific vegetable*

VEGETABLE SOUP: *see* SOUPS

VINEGAR

HAVE ONE KIND, NEED ANOTHER: Vinegars can be substituted for one another, but don't expect the dish to taste as it was intended. Here are some substitution suggestions: For balsamic vinegar, substitute sherry vinegar or red wine vinegar and a bit of sugar. White and red wine vinegar can be substituted for each other. For apple cider vinegar, use white vinegar if you're pickling something or wine vinegar if you're not.

NEED SOME, HAVE NONE: Use twice as much lemon juice as you would have used vinegar.

WAFFLES: *see also* PANCAKES

STUCK TO WAFFLE IRON: The waffle iron has lost its seasoning, if it ever had it. Now, if the waffles separate, you'll need to pry them off the top and bottom of the iron. Sandwich the two halves together with whipped cream and jam and call them Belgian Éclair Waffles. They taste great. When the waffle iron is cool, you'll have to scrub all the stuck-on bits of waffles from the crevices of the waffle iron and brush on cooking oil (corn oil works best). Heat the waffle iron for 10 minutes, turn it off, and let it cool. Then wipe off the excess oil with paper towels and vow never to wash your waffle iron again; just brush any crumbs out at the end of your waffle session.

WALNUTS: *see* NUTS

WATERMELONS

TOO MUCH: Mexican cooks know one of the best things to drink on a hot day. Called *agua fresca* (cold water), it's basically puréed fruit with water and sweetener added. You can start with any fruit, but watermelon (or other melon, or berries, or peaches in season) is particularly good. Remove the rind. Remove the seeds by chopping the melon into smallish pieces and pressing the fruit through a coarse-mesh sieve or colander. Purée the fruit in a blender or food processor, thin it out with water if necessary, and sweeten to taste using some of the simple syrup described under "PIES, Drying Out while Cooking." (This is clearly versatile stuff to keep on hand.) Serve really cold.

Or try the following interesting (but tasty) recipe.

Summer Salad

$^1/_2$ cup thinly sliced red onion
1 tablespoon lime juice
8 cups cubed, seeded
   watermelon
$^3/_4$ cup crumbled feta cheese

$^1/_2$ cup pitted black olive
   halves
$^1/_4$ cup chopped mint
2 tablespoons olive oil
$^1/_4$ cup toasted pine nuts

Place the onion slices in a large bowl with the lime juice and let
stand for 10 minutes. Add the watermelon, feta, olives, and mint.
Drizzle the olive oil over it all and toss to blend. Sprinkle with the pine
nuts.

WELSH RAREBIT (RABBIT): *see* CHEESE, Cooked Cheese
that Is Rubbery, Tough, Stringy

WHIPPED CREAM: *see also* CREAM

DIFFICULT TO WHIP, WON'T WHIP: Thoroughly chill the cream, the bowl,
and the beaters. Make sure that the cream is heavy cream, also called
whipping cream (not half-and-half).

NEED SOME, HAVE NONE: For most uses, you can substitute one mashed
banana beaten with one egg white (beat the egg white stiff first) and
sugar to taste. Or use an emergency whipped cream topping (see
"CREAM, Need Some, Have None").

OLD: If you suspect your cream may be getting old and therefore more
likely to turn to butter when whipped, add $^1/_8$ teaspoon baking soda per
cup of cream before whipping it.

OVERWHIPPED, SEPARATED: If it isn't too far gone and you have some
extra fresh cream, trying adding a bit. Whisk only by hand at this point
though. If that doesn't work, you'll never have whipped cream, but if
you keep on going a bit longer, you'll have delicious homemade butter.
Keep beating until it turns solid, then drain off the liquid and refrigerate until it is hard. Knead it by hand to press out the liquid (which is
whey, so now you know what L.M. Muffet was eating with her curds).

Now you have sweet butter. If you want salted butter, add $^1/_4$ teaspoon salt per pint of cream that you started with and knead some more.

WON'T STAY WHIPPED: If you want whipped cream to look lovely for a long time, as on a cake or other dessert that must sit for a while, dissolve 1 teaspoon gelatin in 2 tablespoons hot milk and beat it into a cup of already-whipped cream.

WIENERS: *see* SAUSAGES

WINE

COLD: If the wine gets too cold, some flavor may have been lost. But you may still find it very drinkable. If not, use it for cooking.

Keep in mind that serving red wine at room temperature really means serving it at *cellar temperature*—not 70°F, but more like 55°F.

SOUR: You can't unsour wine, so let it keep on souring, and eventually you'll have some lovely wine vinegar.

YEAST: *see also* BREAD AND ROLLS, Dough Doesn't Rise

EXPIRED: Old yeast won't get your bread to rise. If in doubt, check the expiration date on the package, and, if you're still unsure, "proof" it by adding a little to warm water with $^1/_2$ teaspoon sugar. If it bubbles, it's still good.

HAVE ONE KIND, NEED ANOTHER: One package ($2^1/_4$ teaspoons) of dry yeast is equal to a 0.6-ounce cake of compressed (fresh) yeast. This is true for either active dry yeast or rapid-rise yeast. Active dry and rapid-rise can also be substituted for each other, although the latter does not need to be dissolved or proofed as the former does. Just add it directly to the dry ingredients.

ZUCCHINI

OVERCOOKED AND SOGGY: There's no going back. You can only go further. Cook it until it's really soft. You're going to make zucchini cream
soup. Make a cup of white sauce with a good glug of sherry in it. Purée
the zucchini (in a blender or a food processor, or even use an electric
mixer if it's *really* soggy) and combine it with the white sauce. Loosen
it to soup consistency with whatever liquid is left over from cooking the
zucchini—cream, milk, or even water. Serve with a little freshly grated
nutmeg and a puddle of crème fraîche in the middle of each serving.

TOO LITTLE: Zucchini combines best with stewed tomatoes, but why
not just slice your limited number into thin rounds and use it as a salad
ingredient? The next problem is actually more common.

TOO MUCH: Home gardeners are wary of the generosity of these plants.
If you find yourself ankle deep in an abundant zucchini harvest, make
zucchini bread. It freezes perfectly, keeps for a year in your freezer, and
is a splendid accompaniment for hot winter beverages.

Farewell Zucchini Bread

1½ cups flour
1 cup brown sugar
2 teaspoons cinnamon
1 teaspoon baking soda
½ teaspoon baking powder
½ teaspoon salt
1 cup shredded zucchini

1 cup chopped nuts, ½ cup
  raisins, or ½ cup chopped
  nuts plus ¼ cup chopped
  dried fruit (optional)
2 eggs, lightly beaten
½ cup vegetable oil
1 teaspoon vanilla extract

Preheat the oven to 350°F. Grease a 9 by 5-inch loaf pan.

In a large bowl, combine the flour, sugar, cinnamon, baking soda, baking powder, and salt. Add the zucchini and the nuts and/or dried fruit, if you're using them. Stir together until the ingredients are well distributed.

In a small bowl, combine the eggs, oil, and vanilla. Add the wet ingredients to the dry ingredients and combine with a few gentle folding motions. Pour the batter into the prepared loaf pan and place in the middle of the oven. Bake until a toothpick inserted into the middle comes out clean, about 1 hour.

Alternatively, this recipe can be made very quickly in a food processor. Dump everything into the bowl and process for 5 to 10 seconds. It'll look lumpy, but that's just fine. Bake as above. Be sure the loaves are cool before you wrap them for freezing.

APPENDICES

APPENDIX A

Burned Foods

When food burns during cooking, you need to do three things:

1. Stop the food from cooking.

2. Separate the unburned parts from the burned.

3. Treat the unburned parts, if necessary, to prevent a burned taste.

Here is how to do each most effectively:

1. Remove the pot from the heat at once. Fill a container bigger than the pot (use the sink if necessary) with cold water and put the bottom of the pot in the cold water. Speed is of the essence. Just removing a pot from the flame doesn't stop the cooking; the cold-water plunge does.

2. Preferably using a wooden spoon, remove all the ingredients that don't cling to the pot and transfer them to another similar container. Be sure you don't scrape the bottom or sides of the pot; remove only what comes out easily. (If you now don't have enough of whatever it is, see the appropriate alphabetical listing of this book under subheading "Not Enough.")

3. Taste the food. It is unlikely that it will have a burned taste, but if it does, cover the pot with a damp cloth and let it stand for about 30 minutes. Taste it again. If the taste is still unpleasantly burned or smoky, your food is probably beyond repair—unless you can take advantage of the smoky taste by adding barbecue sauce and renaming it "country-style" whatever it was.

APPENDIX B

Thawed Frozen Foods

When you defrost frozen foods, either intentionally or accidentally, and you have no need for them right away, most authorities recommend that you do not refreeze; either store them in the refrigerator briefly and use as soon as possible, or throw them out.

The basic question you must now ask yourself is this: how many authorities telling you otherwise would it take to get you to change your mind? One? Ten? A hundred?

We leave this up to you. We do, however, offer the opinion of one reputable authority who says that it is okay to refreeze thawed food. He is Dr. Walter A. Maclinn, a research specialist in food technology at Rutgers University.

Dr. Maclinn says that you can expect foods to be somewhat softer than normal when they are thawed the second time, but otherwise everything is all right. This assumes, of course, that the food did not thaw *and* begin to go bad before you refroze it. The package of green beans that mostly defrosted can go back in the freezer. The leftover clam chowder that warmed to room temperature and smells a little bit suspicious should be thrown out.

APPENDIX C

Too Much Food: How to Store It

This chart gives you an idea of how long leftover foods can survive in the refrigerator or freezer. The times are only approximate, and we make no guarantees, because we don't know how old the food was when you bought it or how close to ideal temperatures your refrigerator performs. (Optimum temperatures are 0°F in the freezer and 34°F to 38°F in the refrigerator.) We tend to be conservative; in most cases, a little bit longer shouldn't hurt. In the Special Notes column, (F) refers to freezer only and (R) to refrigerator only.

KIND OF FOOD	REFRIGERATOR	FREEZER	SPECIAL NOTES
BAKED GOODS			
Bread, cakes, rolls	1 week	2 mos.	Due to sugar content, cake can be kept at room temperature for up to a week.
Cookies:			
Dough	2–3 days	3 mos.	
Baked	2 weeks	4–6 mos.	
Muffins	3–4 days	2 mos.	
Pies	2–3 days	2 mos.	Don't freeze custard pies; they will get watery.
Tortillas	1 week	3 mos.	Wrap tightly.
Waffles, pancakes	1–2 days	1 mo.	

KIND OF FOOD	REFRIGERATOR	FREEZER	SPECIAL NOTES
DAIRY PRODUCTS			
Butter, margarine	1 mo.	6 mos.	Wrap tightly.
Cheese:			
Cottage, ricotta, cream cheese	3–5 days	Do not freeze.	
Other soft cheeses	1–2 weeks	2–3 mos.	
Hard cheeses	3–6 mos.	6 mos.	
Ice cream		2 mos.	
Milk, cream	3 days	Do not freeze.	
EGGS			
Whole, raw eggs	2 weeks	6–8 mos.	(F) Do not freeze in shells. Break into container.
Yolks or whites separated, raw	1–2 days	6–8 mos.	(R) Keep yolks covered with water; whites in covered containers.
Hard-boiled eggs	8–10 days	Do not freeze.	
FISH			
Cod, flounder, haddock, halibut, shrimp	1 day	4 mos.	(R) Wrap or cover loosely. (F) Wrap tightly in freezer wrap and tape well. Use waxed paper to separate individual pieces of fish.
Mullet, ocean perch, sea trout, striped bass, shucked clams	1 day	3 mos.	
Salmon, crab meat	1 day	2 mos.	
Cooked fish, shellfish	1–2 days	3 mos.	Texture of fish may become mushy when defrosted.

KIND OF FOOD	REFRIGERATOR	FREEZER	SPECIAL NOTES
FRUITS			
Avocados	3–4 days	4–6 mos.	See "AVOCADOS, Too Many," for info on how to purée them first.
Bananas	Store at room temp.	4–6 mos.	Will soften in freezer; use for cooking.
Citrus fruits, apples	7 days	Do not freeze.	(R) Store uncovered or in crisper section.
Fruit-juice concentrates	1 week	12 mos.	
Most other kinds	3–5 days	10–12 mos.	(F) Fruits other than berries should be packed in sugar or syrup or syrup plus ascorbic acid (vitamin C).
MEATS			
Beef, roasts, steak	3–5 days	12 mos.	(R) Wrap or cover loosely. (F) Wrap tightly in freezer wrap and tape well. Use waxed paper to separate individual pieces.
Cooked meat	1–2 days	3 mos.	
Ground meat	1–3 days	1–3 mos.	
Lamb chops	2–3 days	6–7 mos.	
Liver, kidneys, tongue	1–2 days	1–3 mos.	
Lunch meats	4 days–2 weeks	1–2 mos.	They lose flavor quickly. Wrap well.
Pork, cured:			
Bacon	7 days	2–3 mos.	
Frankfurters	7 days	1 mo.	
Ham, sliced	3–5 days	1–2 mos.	
Ham, whole	7 days	1–2 mos.	
Pork, fresh	3–5 days	8 mos.	
Rabbit	1–2 days	6–12 mos.	
Sausage:			
breakfast links	1 week	1–2 mos.	
cured	1 mo.	1–2 mos.	
fresh	1–2 days	1–2 mos.	

KIND OF FOOD	REFRIGERATOR	FREEZER	SPECIAL NOTES
MEATS, *continued*			
Veal	3–5 days	6–8 mos.	
Venison	2–4 days	6–12 mos.	
POULTRY			
Chicken, cooked	2–3 days	4–6 mos.	(R) Wrap or cover loosely. (F) Wrap solid pieces tightly in freezer wrap and tape well.
Chicken, pieces	1–2 days	6 mos.	
Chicken, whole	1–2 days	12 mos.	Put cooked juicy dishes in tightly closed, rigid containers.
All other poultry (goose, turkey, duck, etc.)	1–2 days	6 mos.	
SOUPS, STEWS, CASSEROLES	2–3 days	2–4 mos.	(R) See special hint under "SOUPS, Too Much."
TOFU	1 week	5 mos.	(R) After opening, tofu should be stored in water; change the water daily. (F) Freezing causes the texture to become firm and crumbly (some people prefer this texture).
VEGETABLES			
Canned (open); cooked	1–3 days	8–10 mos.	(R) Store canned (open) or cooked vegetables in covered container.
Fresh, above-ground	4–7 days	8–10 mos.	(R) Store fresh vegetables uncovered in crisper section. (F) Boil or blanch before freezing. Do not freeze tomatoes, lettuce, radishes, or any very crisp vegetable.
Fresh, root	1–2 weeks	8–10 mos.	Blanch prior to freezing.

APPENDIX D

The Art of Measuring:
How to Measure and Pour Foods

When you are following other people's recipes, it is usually wise to use standard measuring spoons and cups, since that is what the recipe maker probably used. (There are exceptions: One story is told about a haughty couple who, having dined out, asked that the chef be presented to them. When he appeared, they asked him, cajoled him, finally even bribed him for the secret of his specialty dish. Finally he gave in. A pinch of this, a handful of that, and so on, he related, and finally, "Just before serving, add one mouthful of wine.")

When you measure dry ingredients (flour, sugar, etc.), spoon the ingredient into the measuring container to overflowing and then level it off with something flat, like a knife blade or spatula. When measuring sifted flour, always sift before measuring, and never pack the flour into the measuring cup or spoon; that will unsift it.

On the other hand, moist or dense ingredients, like butter and brown sugar, should be packed firmly into the measuring container.

Sticky ingredients, like honey and molasses, should be poured directly into the utensil; never try to dip the utensil into the container. If you grease the cup or spoon lightly, the sticky stuff won't stick.

Weights and Measures You May Need to Know

A. **EQUIVALENT WEIGHTS AND MEASURES**

1 dash = about $^1/_8$ teaspoon
1 teaspoon = $^1/_3$ tablespoon
1 tablespoon = 3 teaspoons
2 tablespoons = $^1/_8$ cup or 1 ounce of liquid
4 tablespoons = $^1/_4$ cup
$5^1/_3$ tablespoons = $^1/_3$ cup
8 tablespoons = $^1/_2$ cup
16 tablespoons = 1 cup
1 cup = $^1/_2$ pint of liquid
1 pint = 2 cups or 16 ounces of liquid
2 pints = 1 quart
4 quarts = 1 gallon
1 pound = 16 ounces
1 jigger of liquid = $1^1/_2$ ounces = 3 tablespoons of liquid

B. **HOW MUCH OF WHAT WEIGHS HOW MUCH**

Bread crumbs: 1 cup = 4 ounces
Butter: 1 stick = 4 ounces = $^1/_2$ cup
Butter: 4 sticks = 16 ounces = 2 cups
Butter: 1 tablespoon = $^1/_2$ ounce
Rice: 1 cup = 8 ounces
Sugar: 1 cup granulated = 7 ounces
Sugar: 1 cup brown = 7 ounces
Sugar: 1 cup confectioners' = $5^1/_3$ ounces

C. **CAN SIZES**

6-ounce can = $^3/_4$ cup
8-ounce can = 1 cup
No. 1 can = 11 ounces = $1^1/_3$ cups
12-ounce can = $1^1/_2$ cups
No. 303 can = 16 ounces = 2 cups
No. 2 can = 20 ounces = $2^1/_2$ cups
No. $2^1/_2$ can = 28 ounces = $3^1/_2$ cups

How to Pour

Pouring ingredients from one utensil to another is such a simple thing, and yet it so often results in sugar or oil or milk or whatever all over the counter or the floor.

The main thing you should consider when pouring ingredients is using a funnel—not necessarily a fancy store-bought one made of plastic or metal, although those are all right, too, but a homemade, spur-of-the-moment funnel. For example, you carry one around with you all the time: your hand. It takes only a minute of practice to shape your hand into a funnel-like shape though which you can pour liquids or powders.

Or use some paper. Almost any kind of paper, except paper towels, can be rolled up into a temporary funnel—even for liquids. You can pour a whole gallon of liquid through a funnel made from a piece of ordinary writing paper before it starts to get soggy. (Use unprinted paper, if at all possible. Ink is not in any of the basic food groups.) Consider, too, waxed paper and aluminum foil.

Here are two laboratory tricks known to all chemists: To pour powders very accurately from a jar, use a rotating instead of a pouring motion. Slant the jar or box slightly downward so the contents just fail to come out. Now rotate the jar or box back and forth, from left to right, and you will find you have amazingly accurate control over how much comes out.

To pour liquids from a large, unwieldy can in which the hole or spout is not centered (as with big cans of oil, for example), pour with the spout at the top—that is, as far as possible from the container you are pouring into. This results in a steadier flow, less dripping, and a neater cutoff when you stop pouring.

APPENDIX E

Stains

Here are suggestions on how to remove the most common food and food-related stains. On colored fabrics, it is always safest to treat an inconspicuous area before removing the entire stain.

These days, they do make some marvelous stain-removing products (wipes and sticks and such) that you can carry with you, and if you use them as soon as you've made a mess, you are less likely to need this section.

ALCOHOLIC BEVERAGE: Sponge with amyl acetate (banana oil) or cleaning fluid. Launder in hot water and rinse in warm water. Some more specific ideas:

Beer: Blot with warm water and mild detergent. For a more stubborn stain, blot with 1 part white vinegar to 2 parts warm water. Rinse and repeat as necessary.

Wine: Sponge the stain gently. Don't rub it in. Blot using mild detergent or with 1 part white vinegar to 2 parts warm water.

BLOOD: Soak in cold water. Wash in warm water. If the stain remains, soak in ammonia water (2 tablespoons ammonia per gallon of water).

BUTTER: Wash in warm sudsy water. If it's a nonwashable fabric, sponge with a spot stain remover or dry-cleaning solvent.

CHOCOLATE, COCOA: Soak in cold water; sponge in hot sudsy water. Bleach with hydrogen peroxide if necessary. Wash in hot water (warm for colored fabrics).

COFFEE, TEA: Pour boiling water through the stain and then launder normally. If the stain remains, bleach with hydrogen peroxide.

EGG: Soak in cold water, never hot. Launder normally with hot water. For colored fabrics, if colorfast, soak in solution of 2 tablespoons detergent and 1 tablespoon hydrogen peroxide per gallon of water. Launder normally with warm water.

FRUITS: Rinse in cold running water; wash in hot water with detergent. If the stain remains, bleach with hydrogen peroxide.

GREASE ON CARPET: Pour on club soda. Rub with a cloth or damp sponge.

JUICE: Blot with mild detergent and water. Rinse with white vinegar and then with cool water.

KETCHUP, SOY SAUCE: Blot with a diluted mild detergent. Rinse. Blot with 1 tablespoon ammonia mixed with $1/2$ cup lukewarm water. Rinse.

LIPSTICK: Rub with lard and blot until the stain is transferred to the blotter. Wash in hot water (warm for colored fabrics) with detergent. Bleach with hydrogen peroxide if necessary. Or try dabbing with rubbing alcohol.

MEAT, GRAVY: Soak in cold water, never hot. Wash with hot water (warm for colored fabrics) and detergent. Bleach with hydrogen peroxide if necessary.

MILK, CREAM, ICE CREAM: Rinse under cold running water. Wash in hot water (warm for colored fabrics) with detergent.

MUSTARD: Work glycerin in, rub the spot, and then wash in hot water (warm for colored fabrics) with detergent. If the stain remains, bleach with hydrogen peroxide.

SOFT DRINKS: Sponge with equal parts of alcohol and glycerin, or with lukewarm water and alcohol. Launder in hot water (warm for colored fabrics) and detergent.

TOMATO SAUCE: Blot. Rinse under running water. Use gentle detergent and continue to blot and rinse. You can rinse with vinegar.

VEGETABLES: Rinse in cold running water. Wash in hot water with detergent (warm for colored fabrics). If the stain remains, bleach with hydrogen peroxide.

APPENDIX F

Problems with Utensils and Appliances

Look first for the kind of utensil or appliance, like "Pot" or "Grinder," and then for the kind of problem, like "Burned" or "Clogged."

ALUMINUMWARE

DIRTY: Boil apple peels in aluminum pots; it will make cleaning them (the pots) ever so much easier. It's some chemical miracle at work.

STAINED OR DARKENED: Boil 2 teaspoons cream of tartar in 1 quart water for 10 minutes to lighten aluminum.

BAKING STONE

SOAPY TASTING: If you already cleaned your baking stone with soap prior to reading "Stained/Dirty," below, there is hope. Submerge the stone in plain warm water (you may need your bathtub) and soak for 20 minutes. Repeat as needed.

STAINED OR DIRTY: Never use detergent on a baking stone. It will soak in and make your next pizza taste soapy! Scrub with baking soda and water and rinse well.

BLENDER

GUNK STUCK ON IT: Blenders can be hard to clean out, particularly if they have been sitting with food in them. Mix a 1-to-1 ratio of baking soda and water. Let it sit in the blender for half an hour, then run the blender. Rinse.

SMELLY: Same remedy as for "Gunk Stuck on It," above.

BOTTLES

DIRTY: If the bottle brush won't reach or isn't firm enough to remove the gunk, fill the bottle halfway with soapy water and add a handful of pea-size pebbles. Shake vigorously. Save the pebbles to use another time. If you're afraid of breaking the bottle, you might try using split peas or other dried beans instead of pebbles. If you have a sack of those ceramic pie weights, the ones that look like tiny smooth chickpeas, you can use them, too.

SMELLY: Fill the bottle half full with water and add 1 tablespoon prepared mustard or baking soda. Shake well, let stand for 1 hour, then rinse.

CAST-IRON COOKWARE

GREASY: Pour in lots of salt and you can easily wipe up the grease plus the salt with paper towels.

RUSTING: Scrub with steel wool. Or vegetable oil and salt. Or fine-grit sandpaper. *Note:* You will need to scrub. Hard. And reseason the cookware when you're done.

COFFEE PERCOLATOR

STAINED: Does it really matter what the inside of your percolator looks like? If so, fill it with water and add 3 tablespoons baking soda and 1 tablespoon cream of tartar. Let it percolate, then scrub out and rinse.

COFFEE OR TEA STRAINER

CLOGGED: Sprinkle coarse salt in the basket and run under hot water.

CUTTING BOARD

SMELLY: If it's not wood, you can try running it through the dishwasher. Rub it with a sliced lemon or lime. Or rub it with dry mustard, leave for a few minutes, and then rinse

STAINED: Sprinkle your cutting board with some salt, rub with a damp cloth, and then rinse. Some recommend rubbing the salt with a lemon half rather than a cloth. For a stubborn stain, try making the salt into a paste, spread it over the board, and let sit for 24 hours.

DISHES OR PLATES

CRACKED: For hairline cracks, put the plate in a pan of milk and boil for 45 minutes. The crack will usually disappear. If it doesn't, it was probably bigger than you thought.

GREASY: Soak them in hot water to which you've added baking soda. Chemically, baking soda plus grease equals soap. Not soap you'd use on the baby, but nevertheless soap that will clean your dishes.

SMELLY: Wash them in salty water. Or use a little ammonia in hot soapy water. Or add a bit of ground mustard to the wash water.

STAINED: Soak them overnight in hot soda water (that's hot water plus baking soda). Then rub with a vinegar-moistened cloth dipped in salt. This is especially effective on tea stains.

DISHWASHER

SMELLY: Pour a gallon of vinegar in the bottom and let sit for 1 hour. Run the dishwasher on a normal cycle.

STAINED, RUSTY: Pour $1/4$ cup citric acid into the dishwasher and run using the normal cycle. No citric acid? Use powdered orange or lemon drink instead.

DOUBLE BOILER

NEED ONE, HAVE NONE: How many people actually own a double boiler? Luckily, you can make one by filling a pot partway with water and fitting on top of it a metal bowl so that the bottom of the bowl is just above the water level. Heat the water and use the contraption as you would a double boiler.

ENAMELWARE

DIRTY: Fill with cold water plus 3 tablespoons salt. Let sit overnight. Then boil. Then clean (easily).

FOOD PROCESSOR

SMELLY: Mix a 1-to-1 ratio of baking soda and water. Put it in the bowl of the processor and let sit for half an hour. Rinse. Always dry all pieces thoroughly.

FORKS

DIRTY: Try cleaning them with an old toothbrush. (Dirty toothbrush? Try cleaning it with an old fork.)

FREEZER OR FRIDGE

NOT COLD ENOUGH: You've probably heard that you lose 30 minutes of safe cool temperature every time you open the door. Consider putting really perishable things (like cream, which you're likely to use more often) into an ice chest, if you have one.

SMELLY: We assume you mean a persistent bad smell. You've already taken everything out, gotten rid of anything that has gone bad, and washed the whole thing down with soap and/or baking soda? The only thing left to do is turn off the fridge, stuff the whole thing with wadded-up newspaper (leaving all the perishables out, of course), and leave it for a few days.

GARBAGE DISPOSAL

SMELLY: Grind up half a lemon, orange, or grapefruit in it. In fact, never throw a lemon rind out—keep them in quarters in a plastic bag in your freezer and throw one down the disposal whenever it begins to smell funny. Another thing to try is equal amounts of baking soda and vinegar ($1/4$ cup of each). Pour into the disposal and let it sit for a couple of minutes. Flush with hot water. Some people swear by ice cubes. They say grinding the ice cleans off the disposal blades. We have doubts about this method, but one thing's for sure—it certainly does scare the cat!

GLASS BAKEWARE

THINGS STICK TO IT AND BURN: When cooking in glass bakeware, lower the heat by 25°F and increase the cooking time slightly.

STAINED: Scrub with baking soda and water.

GLASSWARE

STAINED: If the stains are coffee stains, make tea in the utensil; the tannic acid of the tea should remove the coffee stains.

STUCK TOGETHER (GLASSES): Put cold water in the top one and sink the bottom one in hot water. They will come apart.

GRATER

COVERED WITH STICKY RESIDUE FROM SOFT CHEESE: Rub with either a hard crust of bread or a potato.

SMELLY: Rub a hard crust of bread over it.

GRIDDLE

SMOKING: This hint alone is worth the price of the book. This may be the most useful hint ever devised. This is the kind of hint that will make you want to drop everything and call up all your friends and relations and share it with them before another minute goes by. Are you ready? All right, here it is: To keep your griddle from smoking, rub it regularly with half a rutabaga. (Applause?)

GRINDER: *see* MEAT GRINDER

HANDS (YOUR VERY OWN)

BURNED: Vanilla extract will help take away the initial pain. So will a good stiff shot of bourbon.

GREASY: Very hot water will generally dissolve and remove most food-type grease. Next time, for greasing baking pans and the like, wear a waxed-paper or plastic-wrap bag as a glove to smear the butter around.

SMELLY: One of the finest household hints devised by man (are you listening, Heloise?) was announced by Hank Weaver on his radio program on KABC in Los Angeles in 1956. It went as follows: "Ladies, to get that ugly onion smell off your hands once and for all, simply rub them with garlic."

Slightly more reputable methods of de-onionizing your hands are the following: 1) wash with cold water, rub your hands with salt, and rinse; 2) rub your hands with celery salt and wash normally; 3) rub with a raw, unpeeled potato; 4) wash with milk, then with cold water; 5) rub with coffee grounds; and 6) splash with mouthwash.

For hands with a fishy odor, dampen them, rub with salt, wash normally, and then rub with a lemon rind. Or rub them with toothpaste, then rinse. (If these don't work, have you considered the possibility that your hands just naturally smell like fish?)

STAINED: There are two ways to get off most fruit and some vegetable stains. One is to rub the stain with a raw unpeeled potato and then wash normally. The other, best for stains from acidic fruits but good for many others as well, is to wash the hands, wipe lightly, strike a match, and cup your hands around the match to catch the smoke. Stains vanish as if by magic, leaving only clean, blistered (if you keep them there too long) hands.

JARS: *see* SCREW-TOP CONTAINERS

KITCHEN

SMELLY: For an inexpensive and delightful kitchen deodorizer, put some orange peel in the oven at 350°F, with the door ajar. If you've got a really powerful odor you need to deal with fast, boil a teaspoonful of cloves in a mixture of 1 cup water and 1/4 cup vinegar—but be careful not to let the liquid boil away, or you'll be dealing with the smell of burned cloves.

KNIVES

RUSTING: Stick them into an onion and leave them there for 30 minutes, then wash and polish them. Wipe them with a very light coating of vegetable oil to keep the rust from returning.

MEAT GRINDER

CLOGGED: Insert crumpled waxed paper and keep grinding away. The paper will force every bit of food through but won't go through itself or jam up the works.

DIRTY: Run a piece of bread through it before you wash it.

MICROWAVE OVEN

SMELLY: Chop half a lemon into four pieces. Put them in a small bowl with 1 cup water and a few whole cloves. Boil for 5 minutes.

Another option is to boil equal parts water and vinegar for a few minutes and then wipe the microwave down with a clean sponge.

STAINED: Fill a microwaveable bowl with hot water, add a spoonful of baking soda, and microwave for 5 minutes. Wipe down the microwave (the steam should have loosened the stains and made them easy to wipe off). Or try making a thick paste with baking soda and water and rubbing it on the stains with a damp cloth.

OMELETTE PAN

STICKY: Presumably you have seasoned your omelette pan following the manufacturer's instructions. Don't use soap and water on it now. Pour a small mound of salt in it and scrub it with a paper towel moistened in cooking oil. Wipe it out with another paper towel. This is actually the best way to clean a wok, too.

OVEN

DIRTY: Sprinkle a combination of salt and cinnamon on any spillovers that occur while baking. Not only does it prevent a burned, smoky smell from filling the house, but you should be able to use a spatula to lift the boil-over in one big ugly piece after the oven cools.

DOES NOT HEAT: Many things that are made in the oven can be adapted to stove-top cooking (assuming the stove top works. If it doesn't, see "STOVE TOP, Does not Heat" for further suggestions). Anything you were planning to roast can be cut up and braised over low heat or sliced thin and sautéed. If you have more things that need cooking or heating than you have burners for, cook things in layers: Put a bowl with cooked food (or something that just needs heating) over a pot boiling something else. Steam vegetables in a colander suspended over a pot with boiling potatoes in it. If you were planning a cake for dessert, turn it into a steamed pudding—which can be basically a cake steamed in a covered bowl. Consult your big cookbook for exact directions.

TEMPERATURE UNKNOWN: How could this possibly happen? Okay—the knob falls apart. If you don't have an oven thermometer to check it, preheat the oven for 15 minutes. Put a sheet of plain white paper on the center rack. Leave it in for 5 minutes. Check the color:

pale biscuit color: 300°F or less
light brown: 350°F to 400°F
golden brown: 400°F to 450°F
deep brown: 450°F to 500°F
black: over 500°F
ashes: don't even use it for pizza!

PANS: *see* POTS AND PANS

PASTRY TIPS

CLOGGED: Metal ones can be boiled clean. Plastic ones must be soaked in hot water. Ream them out with a wooden toothpick or a bamboo skewer.

PITCHER

DRIPPY: If you're sure someone hasn't given you one of those dribble pitchers from the joke shop, you can quell drips by rubbing the top of the lip of the pitcher with a tiny bit of butter. There's a tongue twister in there somewhere, but we can't quite find it.

PLASTICWARE

STAINED: Soak for 20 minutes in a gallon of warm water plus 1 cup bleach. Wipe the plasticware dry and then wash it normally. If this doesn't work, rub the stains with dry baking soda. If that doesn't work, sand the plastic with a very fine grade of silicon carbide paper (the black stuff that feels like sandpaper), making sure the plastic is wet when you sand it.

PLASTIC WRAP

STUCK: Some people, discouraged by the failure of the plastic-wrap people to come up with a product that you can always find the end of when you want it, have taken to keeping their plastic wrap in the refrigerator. Cold plastic wrap is easier to handle and just as effective.

PLATES: *see* DISHES OR PLATES

POTS AND PANS

BURNED: For aluminum, iron, ceramic, Pyrex, and stainless-steel pots and pans, first scrape out what you can with a wooden spoon. Then partly fill with water and a strong detergent or fabric softener. Boil for 10 minutes. Let stand as is overnight. When you pour off the water, the burned part will be cleanable with a scouring pad or steel wool. (Alternatively, add lots of salt to the pot or pan and heat on the stove; the food may "flake" out along with the salt.)

For aluminum pans, this miracle sometimes works: boil an onion in the pan; the burned stuff will detach itself and rise to the top.

If a truly beloved utensil is hopelessly burned, there are professionals who specialize in restoring such items by cleaning them with strong acid and repolishing the metal. This will cost more than buying a new one, but if it's the pot you used to cook the goulash that caused your spouse to propose to you, it may be worth it. Check online for "Metal Finishers." These are the same people who can recoat the inside of heavy copper pans whose lining has worn off over the years. Since good-quality copper pans are exceedingly expensive, their repair often makes good sense.

DIRTY: Some kinds of dirt are best cleaned in cold water, not hot. These include eggs, dough, sauces, and puddings.

GREASY: As you may have read under "DISHES OR PLATES, Greasy," soaking them in baking soda and hot water works best. Chemically, baking soda plus grease equals soap.

RUSTING: This works especially well with cake pans: scour them with a hunk of raw potato dipped in cleaning powder.

SMELLY: Wash them in salt water or in hot soapy water plus a dash of ammonia.

REFRIGERATOR: *see* FREEZER OR FRIDGE

SCISSORS

DULL: Cut a piece of sandpaper into strips. You'll not only have a lovely collection of narrow strips of sandpaper, you'll also have a sharper pair of scissors.

SCREW-TOP CONTAINERS

STUCK: H. Allen Smith revealed to the world the technique for opening all screw-top containers. Now there are untold millions of us who face Mount Kisco, or wherever he lived, and say "thank you" every time we are faced with an obstinate top. The technique? Bang the top *flatly* on a hard surface, like the floor. Not the edge, but the flat surface of the top. Just once. Hard. That's all. And to think of all those jars we used to hold under hot water.

SLOW COOKER

STAINED: There are a variety of options. Fill the slow cooker with warm water, add a couple of denture tablets, and let soak overnight. Or make a paste of cream of tartar and vinegar, apply to the stain, and rinse. Or fill the cooker three-fourths of the way with hot water and add 1 cup white vinegar. Cover and cook on high for 2 hours or overnight on low. Rinse.

STAINLESS STEEL

STAINED: This is like giving instructions for ironing permanent-press fabrics. Nonetheless, if you have rainbow-like stains on your stainless steel, they are permanent; they will never come out. For brownish stains, soak a dishcloth in full-strength ammonia, cover the stain with it for 30 minutes, and wash normally.

STOVE TOP

DOES NOT HEAT: This is often a last-minute discovery that calls for real ingenuity. What else do you have in your household that does heat? Maybe you have a toaster, electric skillet, toaster oven, slow cooker, or deep-fat fryer (which can be used for soup or stews or boiling water—just make sure you clean it well before you use it). Have you a camp stove? Could you use a barbecue or hibachi? Could your fireplace be used? (This is getting adventurous.) Warm bread or rolls in the drying cycle of a dishwasher—being very careful about the setting when you turn it on. And we have been told that it is possible to strap a foil-wrapped chicken to the exhaust manifold of a car and drive until it's done—but as long as you're out in the car, why not head for a restaurant?

TEFLON

STAINED: In the utensil, boil a mixture of 1 cup water, $^{1}/_{2}$ cup bleach, and 2 tablespoons baking soda. Then wash in warm suds. Coat the Teflon with oil before using it.

THERMOMETER

READING TOO HIGH OR TOO LOW: If you're questioning the calibration of your instant-read thermometer, test it. Bring a saucepan of water to a boil and take the water's temperature. It should be 212°F if you're at sea level. Some dial-face thermometers can be recalibrated by adjusting the nut just behind the head; if you have a digital thermometer, you'll just have to remember how many degrees off it is and factor that in each time you use it.

THERMOS BOTTLES

DIRTY: Fill with warm water plus 1 heaping teaspoon baking soda. Let it sit overnight, then clean.

WOODENWARE

WORN OUT: If it's really worth saving, here's how: Sand thoroughly. Then make a mixture of 1 tablespoon mineral oil and $^{1}/_{2}$ tablespoon powdered pumice (from the hardware store). Rub on the wood with cheesecloth until it is dry and smooth—perhaps 30 minutes. Let dry for 24 hours. Remove the dust. Repeat this operation if necessary. It could take ten or twelve times to restore a really battered wooden item. Never, never wax, shellac, or polish a good wooden bowl.

APPENDIX G

How to Repair Thanksgiving Dinner

So you're preparing a festive once-a-year dinner for many more people than you're comfortable cooking for? And you're cooking far more dishes than you'd usually attempt at once and you want them all to turn out perfectly and at exactly the same time? Oh, and you say that some of your guests are folks who make you feel nervous and edgy, like your mother-in-law, your cousin who does everything perfectly, or your aunt who always said you'd amount to no good?

Is this a recipe for disaster or for Thanksgiving dinner?

It's often both.

It's no surprise that Thanksgiving includes its fair share of culinary catastrophes. And while those can provide family stories for years to come, we're here to help prevent stories at your expense.

Here are some tips and tricks to make your Thanksgiving dinner turn out to be one that's talked about for all the right reasons.

Note that we have included items that seem to us to be traditional for a Thanksgiving menu. If your family always has jicama on Thanksgiving, you'll have to look it up in the main section of this book.

And finally, let us mention that there are no entries here for "FOOD, Too Much." It's Thanksgiving—overabundance is part of the event! Besides, all of you know what to do with Thanksgiving leftovers.

BRUSSELS SPROUTS

BLAND: Sauté some mustard seeds with your Brussels sprouts if they can stand a bit more cooking (if you overdo it, see "Overcooked," below) or just sprinkle the seeds on top. Or stir a bit of Dijon mustard into them. A sprinkle of balsamic vinegar is also quite good.

FALLING APART: Remove the loose outer leaves and mark an X on the stalk end of each sprout (that is, the place where it was attached to the Brussels sprout tree, or however they grow) with a sharp knife before cooking. This will help them all cook uniformly and they will be less likely to fall apart before they're done.

NOT ENOUGH: They pair beautifully with carrots. Red onions, too. Roast them together with some olive oil and a little garlic. Glaze with balsamic vinegar if you like that sort of thing.

OVERCOOKED: Heat your oven to 450°F and spread the overcooked sprouts on a baking sheet. Drizzle with a little olive oil and roast them for just a few minutes until brown and crisp. The crispness will offset the softness from overcooking. Or see "BRUSSELS SPROUTS, Overcooked," in the main section of this book for another option.

SMELLY: If you want your house to smell of things in your feast other than Brussels sprouts, try tossing a heel of bread or a hot red pepper into the pot while you cook them. Remove before serving. Consider, however, that Brussels sprouts become smellier the longer they cook. If yours are too smelly, they may be overcooked.

CRANBERRY SAUCE

WON'T JELL: In homemade cranberry sauce, the jelling occurs as a reaction between the pectin and the sugar. The cranberry sauce must boil long enough for this to happen, so start by cooking it longer. If you reduced the amount of sugar in the recipe, add more (or start a new tradition of cranberry soup), because sugar is necessary to get the sauce to thicken. Finally, it's a good idea to cool your cranberry sauce at room temperature, not in the refrigerator. As the sauce cools, the consistency will firm up somewhat.

GRAVY

BLAND: Add something to unbland it. Some ideas: salt, pepper, thyme, savory, a bouillon cube, some Marmite, soy sauce, mustard, wine or sherry, port, or bourbon.

BURNED: Quickly transfer the gravy to a new pot, without touching or scraping the burned part. Taste it to make sure it's okay and continue.

If it tastes burned, you'll have to start over, making a roux with flour and butter and adding broth and seasonings.

FATTY: The fat will generally be on the top. Soak it off with a piece of bread or a paper towel. Or skim it off with a spoon. This will be easier if you chill it first, but most likely you don't have time for that, as everyone is already at the table waiting to eat.

LUMPY: Whisk it well. If that doesn't work, put it through a sieve. As a last resort, run it through a blender or food processor.

NOT ENOUGH TURKEY DRIPPINGS: Very often, a turkey just doesn't produce enough drippings to make the amount of gravy you need. That's okay. Supplement the fat with some butter to make the roux. Then add your broth—homemade, canned, boxed, or made from bouillon. If that makes it too thin, see "Too Thin," below.

SALTY: You'll have to increase the quantity. That's not a bad thing. In our experience, there's always more turkey and potatoes than there is gravy. Add water and thickening (and flavoring) as necessary.

TOO THICK: Keep whisking in broth until the gravy becomes the right consistency.

TOO THIN: You can simmer it uncovered until enough liquid evaporates and the gravy thickens. But since gravy is usually the last thing made before dinner, you probably don't have the time. You need a thickener. You can stir in some arrowroot (1 tablespoon per cup of liquid) or cornstarch (1$1/2$ teaspoons per cup of liquid). In either case, dissolve it in a little cold water, add to your gravy, and stir over medium heat until the mixture boils and thickens. Cornstarch will need to be cooked for a few minutes to improve the taste. You can also whip up a roux of equal parts butter and flour (start with 1 tablespoon of each for 1 cup of gravy), cooked over medium heat until thick and golden. Whisk the roux into your gravy and bring to a boil, stirring until thickened.

GREEN BEANS

BLAND: If you fear in advance that the beans will be bland, put a pinch of sugar in your cooking water. Once they're cooked, you can pep them up with some dill weed or basil. Tossing them with some fat (butter or a nicely flavored oil) and some toasted sesame seeds or toasted slivered almonds is nice and makes them fancy looking, too.

LOSING COLOR: If your beans' color is starting to fade as they simmer, either they're overcooking, in which case you should drain them right away and plunge them into ice water to stop the cooking, or there's lemon juice or vinegar in the water, in which case you should add a pinch of baking soda to balance the acidity.

NOT ENOUGH: Luckily, beans go with so many other vegetables that unless your cupboard is completely bare, you should be able to find something to mix with them. Peas, lima beans, corn, broccoli, cauliflower, red bell pepper, and zucchini will all work. A combination of two or three will look and taste particularly good—as if you meant to do it!.

OVERCOOKED: Overcooked green beans can be made into a soup by puréeing them with broth. You can add cooked carrots or potatoes first if you like. You can add cream. You can even add some basil, thyme, or dill.

Or, if you have the ingredients for it, we recommend turning your overcooked green beans into the classic green bean casserole (which, in our experience, always features some pretty soft beans anyway). Sure, it's retro, but holidays are a time for tradition. Mix your green beans with cream of mushroom soup, top with French fried onions (if you don't have a can, just sauté some fresh onions), then bake at 350°F until hot, 20 minutes or so.

MASHED POTATOES

GLUEY: Put them in a casserole dish, top with dabs of butter (and possibly some grated cheese), and put them in the oven to heat. (If they're already fairly warm, 15 minutes at 350°F will probably do it.) Or make patties and fry them.

LUMPY: If it won't adversely affect the consistency, add some warmed milk or butter to help smooth them out. (Do not add cold dairy; it will make the potatoes gluey!) If you have a ricer, put them through it. A food mill would work as well. In a pinch, a strainer could be employed. A mixer may work to smooth out the texture, but be aware that it, too, may turn your potatoes gluey.

Next time, know that it helps to start your potatoes in cold water so that they cook evenly and will be easy to mash to a uniformly smooth texture. Also keep in mind that starchy potatoes like russets cook up fluffier and mash more readily than waxy potatoes such as Yukon golds.

NOT ENOUGH: If you have first-aid potato flakes that we recommend in the introduction, this is the time to add them. Mixed with some real potatoes, no one will notice the difference. And if you're worried someone will, just add extra butter.

NOT FLUFFY: Add a pinch of baking powder and keep fluffing.

RUNNY: You can place them uncovered in a microwave-safe bowl and microwave for a few minutes on high, stirring after each minute. You can boil a couple more potatoes if you have them, drain them well or place them back in the empty pan for 5 minutes, covered with a dry towel, to allow more moisture to steam out. Now, mash these potatoes into your soupy mashed potatoes. Or you can simply thicken up your wet potatoes with some instant potato flakes.

PUMPKIN PIE

BLAND: You are planning to serve your pie with whipped cream, yes? You may want to flavor your whipped cream. You can use any extract or perhaps coffee, a liqueur, orange or lemon zest, or spices such as cinnamon or ginger. You can also add in a teaspoon of rum or brandy. You can also sprinkle your pie with pieces of something (see "Cracked Top," below, for some good suggestions). (For problems with whipped cream, see "WHIPPED CREAM.")

CRACKED TOP: No one will care. If you care, cover the top of your pie. If you have any extra pie crust, roll it out, cut with small cookie cutters, and bake them until golden brown. Arrange them on top of your pie for a nice-looking dessert. Other tasty options include topping the pie with whipped cream, crushed candy (peanut brittle and toffee marry nicely with pumpkin), a streusel (cooked on a baking sheet), nuts (spiced or caramelized are super), or caramel sauce (which will look nicer if you slice and plate the pie before drizzling it on).

CRUST BROWNING TOO FAST: It's usually the edges that start browning first. Cover them with a thin strip of aluminum foil, shaped to fit.

CRUST TOO TOUGH: If it's already cooked, there's no way to untoughen it. Either you'll just have to tough it out and serve it as is (never apologize!), or, if you think it's not servable, then see "Utterly Ruined," below, for an idea.

UTTERLY RUINED: Is the pie crust blackened? Is the pie all over the floor? One Thanksgiving one of the authors did, in fact, take her pumpkin pie out of the oven with a little too much vigor, thereby flinging dessert clear across the kitchen.

No, we are not recommending serving a pie off the kitchen floor, even if the floor is spotless. But if a portion of dropped pie stays in its dish and is salvageable, scoop the filling into parfait dishes and sprinkle with something you have on hand. The suggestions for topping a cracked pumpkin pie are all good, as would be cookie crumbs (particularly gingersnap), butterscotch chips, and banana. Be inventive.

ROLLS

BLAND: This is a perfect opportunity to make a fancy (but simple) flavored butter. Cream some butter with crushed garlic, minced chives or green onions, or some (preferably fresh) herbs.

If your rolls could stand a little more time in the oven, brush them with some beaten egg and sprinkle with poppy seeds or sesame seeds and put back into the oven for 5 minutes or so.

BURNED: As long as they aren't charred lumps of coal, you can probably salvage them by cutting or grating off the bottoms. If you need to grate the tops as well, brush them with a beaten egg and put back into the oven just to cook the egg. It will become shiny (and cover up your mistakes).

COLD, STALE: If you've baked your rolls early to free up the oven for other things, you probably want to reheat them. You can do this while your turkey is resting. Either dip them briefly in cold water or spray with a spray bottle and put them in a 350°F oven until hot. Alternatively, wrap them in foil and heat for 5 minutes at 450°F. This second option works best for soft rolls.

DOUGH RESISTS SHAPING: If your bread dough is unmanageable and won't hold the form you're trying to shape it in, let it rest for 5 to

10 minutes, covered with a dampened cloth, to allow the gluten in the flour to relax.

STUFFING

BLAND: Sage is the most common stuffing seasoning. If you haven't added any (or not enough), try that. It may also need some (more) salt and pepper. You can also try ginger, thyme, parsley, celery salt, or rosemary. Sautéed onions and celery are also good basic additions. If you feel like being a bit more unusual in your vegetable choice, try carrots, sweet potatoes, or bell peppers. Some people even add fruit to their stuffing (which can be especially nice in a cornbread stuffing). Apples, persimmons, raisins, and cranberries are all possibilities. If you eat meat, crumbled browned sausage or bacon adds a nice flavor. Nuts are good, too.

DRY: Add hot liquid (broth is the obvious choice, but apple juice can be interesting, too) and mix until it's a consistency you like.

SALMONELLA WORRIES: This is a concern if you've cooked the stuffing inside the bird or if you've added eggs to the stuffing. When you take the turkey out of the oven, make sure you test the temperature of the stuffing as well as the turkey. It should be at least 165°F. If it isn't, scoop it out and bake or microwave it until it gets there.

SOGGY: The stuffing that comes out of the turkey is often quite wet. If it's too wet for you, put it into a baking dish and bake uncovered at 350°F for about 15 minutes. If you'd like it a little crispy on top, turn on the broiler for a few minutes.

SWEET POTATOES

BLAND: Mash them with ginger (powdered or fresh) or ginger marmalade. Or add almond or peanut butter, with or without some brown sugar or maple syrup. Or orange juice. Or mashed banana. If you prefer a savory sweet potato dish, mash them with butter and thyme. Or butter and soy sauce (and top with sliced green onions).

NOT ENOUGH: Sweet potatoes pair well with many fruits. You can mix chunks of sweet potatoes with chunks of apples (cooked, perhaps with some brown sugar), and purée them both, if you like. Feel free to use prepared applesauce if you have some. The same thing goes for pears. Or you could layer them with bananas and some brown sugar and cinnamon, splash on some orange juice (rum even), and bake at 375°F until tender (about 45 minutes). Mandarin orange slices are another option.

SWEET POTATO CASSEROLE, MARSHMALLOWS BURNED: This is a common problem. If you have spare marshmallows, your best bet is to scrape off the burned ones (everything underneath is most likely just fine), sprinkle on some new ones, and broil just long enough to make them golden. If you don't have any more marshmallows, you still have options. You can just stir the sweet potato mixture a bit (to mix in the marshmallow goo on top) and serve as is (pretending you were never planning a marshmallow topping anyway). Or you can top the casserole with something else. Marshmallow crème or a meringue spread over the top would work (brown both under the broiler before serving). Or just sprinkle the potatoes with some toasted nuts and drizzle with maple syrup.

TURKEY

STILL FROZEN: We hope you mean *partially* frozen. If you mean fully frozen, you should reschedule Thanksgiving for next Thursday. Just so you know, you should allow your turkey to thaw in the refrigerator (thawing at room temperature poses the danger of poisoning your guests with salmonella) and plan for 1 day for every 5 pounds. A quicker way to thaw a fully or partially frozen bird would be to place your still-wrapped turkey into a sink (or tub, depending on size) of cold water. Do not use warm water. Change the water every 30 minutes. It will take about 30 minutes per pound to thaw a turkey from a frozen-solid state, and less time, of course, if it is partially frozen.

GIBLETS STILL INSIDE TURKEY: If you forgot to remove the giblet packet before putting the turkey in the oven, it's okay. Take it out now. It hasn't done damage to your turkey's edibility.

WON'T FIT IN OVEN: Your eyes were bigger than your oven? You'll just have to cut up your turkey. Separate the turkey into breast and leg pieces and then roast. Or you can butterfly the bird by cutting out the backbone and opening up the body so that it's all on one plane. A disassembled bird will cook faster than a whole bird, though, so you'll probably need to adjust your schedule.

OVEN ISN'T WORKING: You'll have to cook it on top of the stove. Cut it into pieces, brown in oil in a Dutch oven, then add broth, and bring to a boil. Turn down the heat, cover, and simmer until the pieces are fork tender. Deep-frying, of course, is an option as well, but make sure you're not overly stressed by your lack of an oven before playing with large amounts of hot oil.

If your stove isn't working either, you may have to take the turkey outside and grill it. Some people do this with a whole turkey (in a roasting pan). Others cut it into pieces first.

BROWNING TOO FAST: Cover the turkey loosely with foil. You may want to uncover it for the last 30 minutes or so to crisp up the skin.

NOT BROWNING ENOUGH: Of course you want your turkey to look Norman Rockwell perfect. Raising the temperature will help, but you don't want to dry out the bird. You can baste the turkey with a mix of butter and honey or molasses, which will accelerate browning. Or, if you want to avoid sweetness, use teriyaki or soy sauce with your butter. Alternatively, sprinkle the bird with paprika while it's cooking.

DONE TOO SOON: If you miscalculated the time it would take to cook, you want to keep the turkey warm without continuing to cook it. Remove the turkey from the oven, wrap it tightly in aluminum foil, and then wrap in a large towel. Place it somewhere warm or insulated (an empty cooler would be perfect if you have one large enough). It'll keep warm for up to an hour. Now get the rest of your dinner ready!

NOT DONE ON TIME: First, serve your guests more cheese and crackers. Then decide if you want to turn up the oven or cut the bird into smaller pieces that will cook more quickly.

If you increase the oven temperature, you can go as high as 450°F, but cover the turkey with aluminum foil first. You don't want to cook at this high heat for too long, or you'll end up with a dry or burned bird. No more than 2 minutes per pound of turkey weight. Remove the foil near the end to crisp up the skin.

Another option is to cut your turkey in half or separate it into breast and leg pieces and lay the pieces flat. It will now cook much faster. Keep in mind that the breast usually cooks faster than the legs. If it's done, and if the dark-meat fans don't protest, you can serve the breast while the legs and thighs continue to cook.

LOOKS LESS THAN PERFECT: Carve the turkey in the kitchen and present a glorious platter of meat. If you want to present the whole turkey, though, and yours is not picture-perfect, your best bet is to divert the eye. Put it on your prettiest platter. And accessorize! We recommend dolling it up with fruits like pomegranates, oranges, or grapes. Or dress it up with vegetables, either ones you plan to serve as side dishes or decorative leafy greens (just make sure you use greens that are hardy enough to stand up to the heat of the bird, like kale; don't use iceberg lettuce or baby arugula!). If you have fresh herbs, sprigs of them tucked here and there look gourmet.

DRY: To help prevent dryness, make sure you let your turkey rest for 20 to 30 minutes after it comes out of the oven. This will give the juices time to settle and redistribute, so they don't run out as you carve.

If it's dry after resting and carving, you do have other options.

Even if your turkey breast is dry, chances are the dark meat is fine, as it takes much longer to dry out. Slice the breast and put it in a baking pan. Bring some broth to a boil and cover the meat with it. Cover the pan with foil and put in a 300°F oven for about 10 minutes. Although the meat will be more moist now while it is warm, it will dry as it cools, so you'll want to serve it immediately. With lots of gravy.

For an easier fix (perhaps for a less dry turkey), you can put some warm broth in a spray bottle and spray the pieces as you carve. (In this case, it's better if you carve in the kitchen; you don't want to have to explain to guests what you're doing.)

Next Thanksgiving, keep in mind that some people flip their turkeys upside down for half of the roasting time because they think that this keeps the breast moister.

RAW: So you completely forgot to put the turkey in the oven? The fastest way to cook it now is to cut it into pieces, brown them on the stove top in a bit of oil until the skin is crisp, and then bake them in a 350°F oven until done (in about 1 hour or so, fingers crossed).

APPENDIX H

A Last-Resort Meal for Four

So, here we are after two hundred and some pages and surely you think, "I can fix anything!" But perhaps not. There may come a time in the life of even the most resourceful chef when she realizes, yes, all *is* lost—the meal is ruined. It is unrecoverable, and one must turn to the last resort. "But wait! What is the last resort?" Take a deep breath; we've thought of everything. Here is a quite satisfactory meal for four persons, made up entirely of items from the "first aid" list that begins on page 8. It should take about 30 minutes from the time you discover your regular dinner is ruined until you sit down at the table to impress your guests with a gourmet feast.

MENU
Pasta Puttanesca
Artichoke Heart Salad
Brownies

Yes, it's just pasta, but first of all you're going to use angel hair pasta, which seems fancier than plain ol' spaghetti. (But if spaghetti is what you have, by all means use that. Or any other pasta you have.) And you're topping it with puttanesca sauce, which not only tastes delicious, it's fun to say. Furthermore, its name has some interesting stories associated with it, which can be explained to your hungry guests as they wait to eat. (Or not, depending on their sensibilities.)

Briefly, pasta puttanesca translates as "whore's pasta." There are a number of stories about how this name originated. One refers to how quickly the dish can be made between clients, another to how it can be made with things already in the larder—emergency dinner, anyone?—because during the 1950s prostitutes from state-run Italian brothels were not welcome at the local markets except at particular times.

You'll be serving pasta puttanesca (made without the traditional anchovy fillets; if you have some in your pantry, by all means, throw in one or two) with a nice artichoke salad. Sorry, we don't know anything salacious about artichokes (feel free to make something up).

And for dessert? Homemade brownies made only with pantry ingredients. And we've included options for making them more interesting, too.

Pasta Puttanesca

1 tablespoon olive oil
4 cloves garlic, minced, or
  1¹/₂ teaspoons garlic
  powder
1 can (28 ounces) puréed
  tomatoes
¹/₂ teaspoon red pepper
  flakes
¹/₂ teaspoon dried basil
¹/₂ teaspoon dried oregano
1 pound angel hair pasta
  (capellini)
1 cup pitted black olives,
  halved or sliced (kalamatas
  are best, but others will do)

3 tablespoons drained
  capers
¹/₄ cup white wine or broth
  (broth made with a bouillon
  cube is fine)
¹/₄ cup tomato paste, if
  needed to thicken the
  sauce
¹/₄ cup chopped parsley (but
  only if you happen to have
  some in the garden or the
  refrigerator)

Artichoke Heart Salad

2 cans (14 ounces each)
  quartered artichoke hearts
¹/₄ cup oil-packed sun-dried
  tomatoes, drained and cut
  into strips

2 to 4 tablespoons vinaigrette

Brownies

2 cups all-purpose flour

2 cups sugar

¾ cup unsweetened cocoa
powder

1 teaspoon baking powder

1 teaspoon salt

1 cup water

1 cup vegetable oil, plus oil
for greasing the pan

1 teaspoon vanilla extract

PREPARING THE MEAL

Preheat the oven to 350°F.

Heat the olive oil in a saucepan over medium heat and add the garlic. When it becomes fragrant, after just a minute or so, add the tomatoes, pepper flakes, basil, and oregano. Bring to a boil, then reduce the heat to low and leave the sauce to simmer, uncovered so it will thicken a bit.

Fill a large pot with water and set it over high heat.

Drain the artichoke hearts and slice them lengthwise into thin slices. Put the slices in a bowl. Toss the sun-dried tomatoes and vinaigrette with the artichokes. Put the bowl into the refrigerator.

Check your sauce and make sure it's simmering. (Turn the heat up or down as necessary.) Give the sauce a stir.

In a large bowl, mix together the flour, sugar, cocoa, baking powder, and salt (a whisk is great for this).

Is your water boiling yet? If so, put your pasta in. And while you're at the stove, give your sauce another stir.

Add the water, oil, and vanilla to the bowl with the flour mixture. Stir. Grease a 9 by 13-inch baking dish and pour in the brownie batter. Put in the oven and set your timer for 25 to 30 minutes for fudgy, gooey brownies; 35 to 40 minutes if you'd like them more solid. A toothpick inserted into the center should have some gooey bits clinging to it for fudgy brownies and be clean for cakelike brownies.

Check your pasta. If it's done, drain it in a colander. Add to your sauce the olives, capers, and wine or broth. If you'd like it a little thicker, stir in the tomato paste.

Plate the pasta and ladle the sauce to cover. If you're using the parsley, sprinkle it on top. Serve with the artichoke salad.

At some point during dinner, you will have to get up and take the brownies out of the oven. Let them sit for at least 10 minutes before cutting.

Serve dessert.

Congratulations. You have just survived a dinner disaster.

Notes on brownies: The recipe can be halved and made in an 8-inch square pan if you prefer. (Though why anyone would prefer fewer brownies we're not sure.)

Adding $1/2$ to $3/4$ cup chocolate chips makes delightfully decadent brownies.

Using coffee instead of water will make these even richer. Substituting one-fourth to one-half of the oil with applesauce will make them less rich (and less filled with fat and calories), but they will still be delicious.

If plain old brownies don't seem exciting enough, do you have any ice cream? We believe it's always a good idea to have some in your freezer. And if that's not enough, how about some fruit? Do you have those frozen berries we mention in the emergency list? A brownie served with vanilla ice cream and blackberry sauce feels very adult. You want to be even more adult? How about a splash of liqueur over your brownie sundae? Coffee liqueur and Irish Cream are both nice, but a good whiskey is also an unexpected treat. Or, go in the other direction and make your inner child happy: dollop chocolate syrup on top. Add a sprinkle of nuts if you have some.